LANGUAGE HANDBOOK SERIES

FRANK A. RICE, GENERAL EDITOR

ARABIC LANGUAGE HANDBOOK

MARY CATHERINE BATESON

CENTER FOR APPLIED LINGUISTICS : 1967

INTRODUCTION TO THE SERIES

Each volume in the Language Handbook Series is intended to provide
an outline of the salient features of a particular language and a
summary of the language situation and language problems of the
country or area in which it is spoken. The scope of the series is
the major modern languages of Asia and Africa.

It is hoped that the handbooks will prove useful to several
different kinds of readers. One is the linguistic specialist who
is not himself a specialist in the particular language treated,
e.g. a Swahili scholar who is interested in Arabic. Another is
the student who is past the beginning stages of his study and who
wishes to have a concise and condensed general picture of the language and its setting. A third reader is the area specialist,
e.g. a sociologist, who wishes to know basic linguistic or socio-
linguistic facts about the area. The handbooks are not designed
to serve as instructional materials for the language in question,
nor are they intended as a guide to local customs or cultural
differences or the like.

There has been some attempt to hold the handbooks to a suggested general framework so as to give the series some uniformity,
but in practice the individual studies vary considerably, both
because of the differences of approach of the individual authors
and the range and variety of problems of the individual languages.
In general, each author in his own way treats the following matters:
the language in its social and historical setting, its linguistic
structure, its writing system (as appropriate), its points of contrast with English, and its literature. The description of the
linguistic structure has provided the greatest problem in presen-
tation. The authors have made a serious effort to avoid excessive
use of technical linguistic terminology but nevertheless a certain
amount of linguistic sophistication on the part of the reader must
be assumed. Given the status of modern linguistics as a discipline

it has not seemed wise to attempt to write in a popularized style.

The language handbooks represent a new kind of venture in the field of applied linguistics. It is probable that some portions or aspects of the various studies will be found inadequate or of little value, but the authors and the editor are confident that the series as a whole represents a useful step in the application of linguistic knowledge to practical language problems.

Frank A. Rice
Director, Office of Information and Publications
Center for Applied Linguistics

ARABIC LANGUAGE HANDBOOK

PREFACE

THIS HANDBOOK is designed to give the kind of information about
Arabic which will be useful to a student of the language, a
specialist in the region where Arabic is spoken, or a linguist
interested in learning about the structure and use of one of the
world's principal languages. Part of the handbook (Chapter 1)
is devoted to explaining what Arabic is like. All the important
features of the grammar are discussed, but they are arranged to
demonstrate how the language functions rather than to teach students how to manipulate it. The remainder of the book is devoted
to describing the use of Arabic: how it has been used for speech
and writing since our earliest records of it and how it is used
today in the modern Arab world where new governmental structures
and technologies are being adapted.

Modern Arabic has eighty million speakers and is the language of more than a dozen states. Historically, Arabic has been
one of the great languages of civilization, accompanying Islam
across North Africa and down the coast of East Africa, up into
Central Asia and across Southeast Asia as a liturgical language,
preserving Greek science through the Middle Ages, and developing
a rich literary tradition with which Europe is mainly familiar
in one of its popular forms, the Arabian Nights. Formally,
Arabic is totally unrelated to English and is the most important
member of the Semitic group of languages with an intricate and
unfamiliar structure.

The use of Arabic is involved with a special social situation which must be understood in order to deal with the area:
the Classical language, which was the vehicle of Islam and of
the literature and is the primary written form today, is relatively uniform throughout the Arab world and across the Islamic centuries, but has never been the ordinary spoken language of the
Arabs. Colloquial Arabic is the language of normal conversation,

but it varies in ways which reflect all the geographical, social, and religious heterogeneity of the population. This situation is called diglossia and presents problems both for description and for the Arabs themselves. Chapter 2 describes the development of Classical Arabic up to the modern period and Chapter 3 describes modern developments in Classical Arabic, its present use in relation to the colloquial dialects, and the origins and structures of the dialects.

Since this is a handbook and not a scholarly volume, references have been kept to a minimum. A bibliography has been included at the end which contains works in English which would be useful as further reading on the topics dealt with here. Many of the items in the bibliography, such as Wright's Grammar and Nicholson's History of Arabic Literature, have been extremely useful in preparing this handbook but are not generally acknowledged. Notes have been inserted in the text only for highly specific material or examples taken from sources which are not mentioned in the general bibliography. On the other hand, the bibliography itself has been designed to include references to books with longer and more specialized bibliographies for more advanced work.

M.C.B.
Harvard University
December 1964

NOTATIONS

All linguistic citations of Arabic material are given in a pho-
nemic transcription (see 1.2). Roots are underlined; all other
material is enclosed within slant lines. Where attention is
directed to some phonetic detail the material is enclosed within
square brackets. For Arabic words and phrases that are not cited
as linguistic examples a more conventional transcription is used.

SYMBOLS AND ABBREVIATIONS:

/ /	encloses phonemic transcription
[ ]	encloses phonetic transcription
' '	encloses glosses or translations
-	indicates a point of affixation
ₒ	indicates division of a linguistic form at the end of a line
*	indicates a hypothetical or reconstructed form
>	'developed to, became' (historical change)
<	'developed from' (historical change)
→	'appears as, becomes' (grammatical process)
←	'results from' (grammatical process)
~	'alternates with; or'
C	a consonant
v	a vowel
$\bar{v}$	a long vowel
ɣ	a semivowel (w or y)
C_1, C_2...	identifies position of C in a root or word
ClA	Classical Arabic
CoA	Colloquial Arabic

xi

TABLE OF CONTENTS

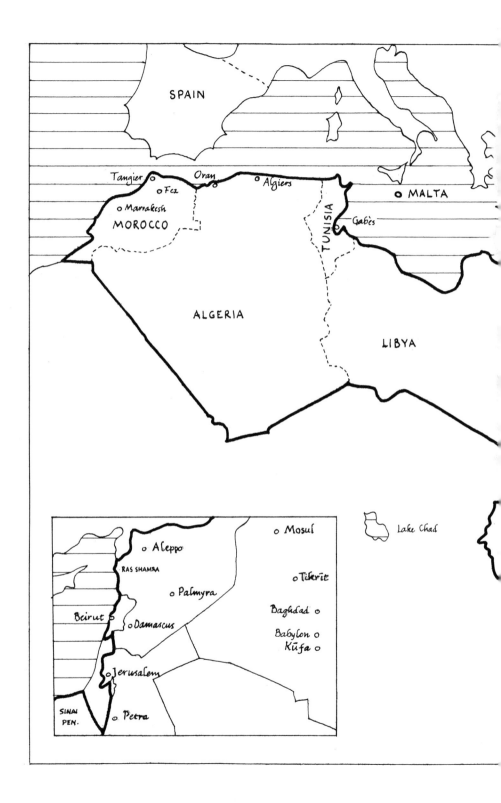

SPAIN

Tangier o   Oran   o Algiers   o MALTA
o Fez
o Marrakesh
MOROCCO   TUNISIA   Gabès

ALGERIA

LIBYA

Lake Chad

o Mosul
o Aleppo
RAS SHAMRA
o Tikrit
o Palmyra
Baghdad o
Beirut
o Damascus   Babylon o
Kūfa o

o Jerusalem

SINAI
PEN.   o Petra

1. AN OUTLINE OF ARABIC STRUCTURE

1.1 General features

Before launching into a systematic sketch of the linguistic structure of Classical Arabic, it seems worthwhile to provide a general
outline of the derivational processes which characterize Arabic,
and which are more highly developed in Arabic than in other Semitic
languages.

Arabic operates by what is known as the 'root and pattern system', which is the hallmark of the Semitic languages and their
most striking feature. Roots usually consist of three consonants,
e.g. klm. These consonant sequences, unpronounceable in themselves, have one or sometimes several general meanings: the root
klm means something to do with speech. Roots cannot be used, however, unless they are provided with vowels, and may be specifically
defined only when in association with a particular vowel pattern,
e.g. /kalimah/ 'word, utterance, maxim', utilizing the pattern
$C_1aC_2iC_3ah$, where $C_1C_2C_3$ represent the three consonants of the root
in relation to the surrounding vowels. Some patterns require the
lengthening (gemination) of one of the root consonants: /kallam/
'he addressed (someone)' has the pattern $C_1aC_2C_2aC_3$. Some patterns
involve the affixation of additional consonants: /kalmāniy/ 'eloquent, fluent speaker', from the pattern $C_1aC_2C_3āniy$, or /muta∘
kallim/ 'spokesman, theologian', from the pattern $mutaC_1aC_2C_2iC_3$.
These patterns, while not perfectly systematic, do in many cases
have clearly definable functions, and the attempt to define these
functions makes up a great part of the grammatical study of Arabic,
whereas the listing of roots is essentially the business of the
dictionary. If this aspect of Arabic structure were perfectly
systematic, the lexicographer would only need to list the roots,
and the speaker could combine them at will with the desired pattern to express, e.g. 'the place where such and such takes place',
'a professional practitioner of such and such', 'one who pretends

1

to be such and such', etc. Unfortunately, this is not the case, and the exploration of an Arabic dictionary is a disillusioning business.

The dictionary is arranged by roots according to the order of the consonantal alphabet, but must spell out in each case what semantic content does in fact result from the combination of a particular root and a particular pattern. The bewildering meanings given in the dictionary for forms that ought to have been predictable may be assigned to several causes: (a) the association of the root with more than one area of meaning: the root klm has a number of forms which refer to wounds and wounding; (b) a cultural and historical understanding of a particular concept which may escape the Western student: the meaning 'theologian' for /mutakallim/ would probably fit in this category; in such cases the meanings seem unrelated and arbitrary in English but are at least to some degree systematic; (c) a series of historical accidents which must be explored for each word: for instance, the use of a particular word which ought to mean either 'maternal' or 'popular, pertaining to the people or nation', for the meaning 'illiterate', may be traced to the readiness of the Muslim theologians to accept a farfetched derivation in order to find a verse of the Qur'ān which proved that Muhammad had not known how to read. However, it is probably more accurate to think of the specificity of particular patterns as a graduated characteristic which has increased slowly by the application of analogy, so that the root and pattern system may be more symmetrical in Arabic than it was in Proto-Semitic.

In dealing with the root and pattern system, it may be helpful to consider that: (a) most patterns, even in what are called pausal forms (see 1.24), provide some information about the place of a particular form in the system of parts of speech, e.g. as a verb form or a noun form; (b) many patterns are the result of a series of derivational steps, some of which are semantically systematic, while others seem arbitrary: the meanings of derived forms of the verb are often startling, though the participles derived from those

2

verb forms stand in a predictable relationship to them; (c) some forms are almost totally predictable, and, if the form does not already exist, will be given a predictable meaning when coined, up to the point where some historical accident intervenes. Accordingly, the discussion of derivation (see 1.3) will be, to some extent, an idealized one, presenting generalizations which may not hold up in practice.

1.2 Phonology

1.21 Consonants

The Arabic writing system is in many ways a fair reflection of the linguistic facts of the language. It contains 28 signs, each of which represents a consonant which may act as one of the three consonants of a root. Since there is some variation in the pronunciation of the consonants in different parts of the Arabic-speaking world, even in formal reading, transcriptions have been chosen which seem to reflect the internal structure of the phonological system (see Table 1). The so-called 'emphatics' of Arabic, which tend to produce a lowering of the vowels in their immediate vicinity, are grouped together in the center column, along with other consonants which may have a similar effect, even though there is no other set of consonants formed in that part of the mouth which do not affect the vowels.

Such a scheme must be qualified in a number of ways.

The emphatics, which are generally velarized, or articulated farther to the back of the mouth than the non-emphatics, vary considerably, even in their formal pronunciation. They were probably all voiced at one time:

Modern pronunciation:	Early Arabic voiced emphatics:	
ض /ḍ/	[ẓ^λ]	lateralized dental fricative
ط /ṭ/	[ḍ]	dental stop
ظ /ẓ/	[d̲]	interdental fricative
ص /ṣ/	[ẓ]	dental spirant

Thus in Early Arabic there was a voiced emphatic corresponding to each voiced-voiceless pair of dentals and interdentals. A

Table 1

The Consonants of Classical Arabic

	PLAIN CONSONANTS		EMPHATIC AND EMPHATIC-LIKE CONSONANTS		SONANTS
	voiced	unvoiced	voiced	unvoiced	
Labial	b ب	f ف			m م w و
Interdental	d̲ ذ	t̲ ث			
Dental	d د	t ت	ḍ ض	ṭ ط	
	z ز	s س	ẓ ظ	ṣ ص	
					n ن
Lateral			(ḷ)		l ل
Trill					r ر
Palatal	j ج	š ش			y ي
		k ك			
Velar			ġ غ	x خ	
Uvular			q ق		
Pharyngeal			ʕ ع	ḥ ح	
Glottal		ʔ ء			
		h ه			

similar relationship may once have existed between /j/, /k/, and /q/: /j/, which is pronounced as either [ž] or [dž], corresponds to the [g] of other Semitic languages; /q/ was originally voiced, and is still so in all modern Bedouin dialects. Some remnants of the earlier pronunciation of the emphatics may be found in Arabian dialects and in the related Semitic languages grouped as South Arabic (see 2.1).

The emphatic [ḷ] does not appear as a letter of the alphabet, but it seems clear that it must be given the theoretical status of a separate phoneme, although it is easier in dealing with Classical Arabic to specify the contexts in which it occurs, i.e. in some contexts in the name of God[1].

It is worth noting some of the limitations on the occurrence of the consonants. Only a small number of them—/m w t s n y ʔ/— may appear as derivational and inflectional affixes, along with / l h d̲ k/, which are used quite extensively in different derivational processes in the system of particles. The emphatics and the less familiar back consonants are almost completely limited to the lexicon of triliteral roots. All of the consonants may be doubled, but there are limitations, in some morphological contexts, on the appearance of the same consonant twice with only a short vowel intervening: $-C_2 v C_3$, when $C_2 = C_3$, tends to become $-(v)C_2 C_3$, if the remaining structure allows. Regardless of root affiliation, initial $*ʔv ʔ- \rightarrow /ʔ\bar{v}-/$, and there are sporadic cases described in the classical grammars of the reduction of /tata-/ to /ta-/, etc. In the formation of roots, $C_2 = C_3$ is common, but C_1 and C_2 are never identical.

In Proto-Semitic, verbal roots appear not to have been formed from consonants produced in the same region of the mouth. Although there has been some shift in articulation, this still means that members of the following classes tend not to occur side by side: the back consonants and the palatals (except /š/ and /y/); the dental and interdental stops and fricatives (with /š/); the liquids; and the labials /f b m/ (but not /w/)[2].

1.22 Vowels

The newcomer to Arabic is often aware of a great variation in the vowels, most of which is automatically produced by the consonantal environment. The basic vowel system consists of three vowels /a i u/ with their corresponding long forms /ā ī ū/, although some ancient forms of Arabic seem to have had a fourth long vowel /ē/ in some positions of modern /ā/, whose occurrence is referred to as imāla 'inclination [of the ā toward the ī]'. There is some controversy over the most illuminating analysis of the long vowels and of the diphthongs /aw/ and /ay/. The Arabic orthography treats the long vowels /ī/ and /ū/ as combinations of a short vowel (supplied by the reader) and a semivowel, i.e. as diphthongs /iy/ and /uw/, analogous to /ay/ and /aw/—while for long /ā/, the

orthographic sign called <u>alif</u> is used to represent the lengthening element. This procedure has a partial grammatical justification in that /y/ and /w/ often enter into the word as root consonants and act phonetically as the second element of a diphthong
whose first element is /a/, or of a long vowel to which a preceding /i/ or /u/ assimilates: iy, uy → /ī/; uw, iw → /ū/; but
this is balanced by the many cases in which no defensible nota-
tion will indicate the process by which a semivowel has been absorbed: awa → /ā/. In the present analysis, the symbolizations
/ā ī ū ay aw/ have been used, but morphological processes may
sometimes result in /iy/ or /uw/, which must then be considered
identical with /ī/ and /ū/.

The strict limitations on the environments within which grammatical /y/ and /w/ can retain their phonological value and the
ramifications of their behavior produce the system of 'weak'
nouns and verbs which causes such difficulty to the student.
/w/ may be followed by any vowel at the beginning of a word, while
initial /y/ cannot precede /i/. Either, if preceded by the corresponding short vowel or short /a/, may be followed only by a consonant, a long vowel, or a short /a/; and if the /y/ or /w/ is a
consonant of the root it is generally eliminated between two short
/a/'s. After a consonant, the sequence semivowel + vowel generally
yields a long vowel, and after /ā/, a single semivowel often becomes /ʔ/. When impossible sequences would occur, such as *iwu or
*ūyi, they are resolved in a number of different ways, depending on
the morphological context.

1.23 Syllable structure

Arabic is a language in which meaningful contrasts depend on both
vowel and consonant length. Two basic syllable types are per-
mitted, with a third, aberrant type in special cases.

All Arabic syllables must begin with a single consonant; the
simplest type is Cv, a consonant plus a short vowel, e.g. /huwa/
'he', /šariba/ 'he drank', with two and three short syllables
respectively. A long syllable either contains a long vowel, Cv̄,
or has the form CvC where another syllable with its own initial

6

consonant follows. For example, /qablī/ 'before me' has a first
syllable of the type CvC (qab-) and a second syllable Cv̄ (-lī),
but since, as has been pointed out above, /lī/ could be written
/liy/, these two ways of forming long syllables in Arabic are
essentially equivalent. Syllables of the type Cv̄C are termed
overlong and rarely occur.

On the whole, syllable formation is very regular in Arabic,
though the handling of weak roots (containing /y/ or /w/) is
complicated by the fact that after their forms have been
simplified to remove impossible vowel sequences, their syllabic
structure must also be brought in line, e.g. *mašay- + -at →
*mašayat → *mašāt → /mašat/ 'she walked'.

Under certain conditions, a cluster of consonants may be grammatically formed at the beginning of a word (if the word has the
definite article, or is an imperative of the first form of the
verb, or is an imperative, a perfect, or a verbal noun of some
of the derived verbs). If such a word is preceded by a word
ending in an open syllable, the two words are run together in
pronunciation: /fawqa/ 'above' + /lbayt/ 'the house' → /fawqal∘
bayt/. Such examples are normally written as separate words in
the Arabic orthography. If the word is preceded by a word ending
in a consonant—there are relatively few cases in which this can
happen—an anaptyctic vowel is supplied: /a/ if the first word is
/min/ 'from': /mina lbayt/ 'from the house'; /u/ if the last syllable of the first word is a pronominal suffix ending in /-um/:
/wajadtumu lbayt/ 'you (masc. pl.) found the house'; and /i/ in
all other cases: /wajadati lbayt/ 'she found the house'. If the
consonant cluster appears after silence, both an anaptyctic vowel
and a consonant (always a glottal stop) must be supplied, i.e.
*CCv → *vCCv → ʔvCCv. This anaptyctic vowel is always /a/ for
the definite article: /ʔalbayt/ 'the house'; and /i/ for verbal
forms and elsewhere, unless the vowel following the cluster is
/u/, in which case it is also /u/; the anaptyctic vowel is not
indicated in isolated citations in this study. When loans from
other languages are assimilated into Arabic, they are altered

to fit this pattern: /ʔiqlīm/ 'climate', /faransā/ 'France'.

1.24 <u>Stress and pausal forms</u>

Classical Arabic has two further phonological features which de-
serve mention, although the one is automatic and the other stylistic and thus do not play the role of distinguishing meanings.

Stress in ClA is automatically produced by the syllable structure of the word: the stress falls either on the long syllable
nearest to the end of the word (except for the final syllable),
or on the first syllable: /kátaba/ 'he wrote', /katábta/ 'you
(masc. sing.) wrote,' /takátabā/ 'the two (masc.) corresponded'.
A major deviation from this rule occurs in many pronunciations of
ClA, where, in words with an initial long syllable followed by
three short ones, the stress may not be more than three syllables
from the end of the word: /maktabatun/ 'library' may be stressed
on either the first or the second syllable. Changes in syllable
structure in the dialects have produced instances, although not a
great many, in which stress distinguishes meaning.

The standard style of reading ClA includes a set of conventions
for dropping final short vowels and dropping or shortening the
case endings at the end of phrases or in isolation where words
appear in 'pause form'. These conventions appear to be part of
the rhyme structure of even very early poetry, and since the system of case inflection constitutes one of the main differences
between ClA and all the colloquials, many speakers of Arabic extend the use of pause forms as much as possible in their use of
Classical.

In the pause forms, which will generally be used for citations
in this study when case or modal endings are not in question, all
words are stripped of the final /-n/ which follows the case ending on indefinite nouns and the case ending itself or any final
short vowel, and the feminine ending is reduced from /-at-/ to
/-ah/ (often pronounced /-a/). The exception to this rule is the
final /-an/ of the indefinite accusative, which becomes /-ā/ or,
in less formal usage, is retained, as it will be in all citations
here. Examples of context forms: /maktabatun/ 'library' (indef.

8

nom.): /baytan/ 'house' (indef. accus.): /lmutakallimu/ 'the
theologian' (def. nom.): these same forms would be realized in
pause as /maktabah/, /baytā/ ~ /baytan/, and /lmutakallim/
(/ʔalmutakallim/, with the initial cluster resolved).

1.3 The noun

The Arab grammarians have traditionally dealt with Arabic in terms
of only three classes of words: nouns, verbs, and particles. This
analysis will be retained here, except that the pronouns will be
included with the particles, roughly defined as the class of words
(except unassimilated loanwords) which resist efforts at analysis
in terms of the root and pattern system. Adjectives are not
formally distinct from nouns, and there is no separate class of
adverbs.

For both nouns and verbs, a discussion of the inflectional system, which operates primarily but not exclusively by affixation,
will precede a discussion of the derivational systems, which involve the total rearrangement of the vowels in their relations to
the root consonants—the imposition of new patterns. While there
is some similarity between the two inflectional systems—each expresses some of the same obligatory categories in slightly varying
ways—a more tangled path must be followed to deal with the derivational systems: nouns derived from simple verbs are included in
the initial discussion of noun derivation, whereas nouns derived
from derived verbs are discussed in relation to the verbs themselves.

1.31 Noun inflection

Arabic nouns are inflected for case, determination, gender (masculine and feminine), and number (singular, collective, dual, plural).

1.311 Case and determination

The role played by Arabic nouns in the sentence is usually indicated by short vowel suffixes: there are three cases, traditionally
referred to as the nominative, genitive, and accusative, but their
functions are not precisely those we generally associate with these
terms. For the majority of indefinite Arabic nouns, these short

vowels are followed by a final /-n/, not indicated on the cursive
line, called 'nunation'. The definite article is the commonest
way of determining a noun; this is /l-/ prefixed to the noun and
assimilated to any initial apical consonant: / t d̲ t d s z ṭ ḍ ṣ
ẓ n l r š/. These are called by the Arab grammarians 'sun-
letters', all other consonants being 'moon letters': /l-/ + /šams/
→ /ššams/ 'the sun', in contrast with /lqamr/ 'the moon'. This is
a morphologically conditioned assimilation whose domain has, however, been expanded to include various other grammatical juxta-
positions of /l/ and these consonants in some dialects.

Nouns also become definite when followed by a determining complement, which may be a noun in the genitive: /baytu lmaliki/ 'the
king's house'; or a suffixed pronoun: /baytu-hu/ 'his house'.
They do not then have nunation or the definite article.

Context forms:

	Definite: 'the house'	Indefinite: 'a house'
Nominative	/lbaytu/	/baytun/
Genitive	/lbayti/	/baytin/
Accusative	/lbayta/	/baytan/

All nouns (except duals and 'sound plurals') follow this regular
declension in the definite, but some distinctions may be lost because the final short vowel of the word base is followed by $C_3 =$
/y/ or /w/ which has been changed into /y/ in the process of derivation, as frequently occurs.

If the vowel before the /y/ is /u/ or /i/, the theoretical
forms are simplified as follows (root qḍy):

	Definite: 'the judge'	Indefinite: 'a judge'
Nominative	*lqāḍiyu → /lqāḍī/	*qāḍiyun → /qāḍin/
Genitive	*lqāḍiyi → /lqāḍī/	*qāḍiyin → /qāḍin/
Accusative	/lqāḍiya/	/qāḍiyan/

(Note that all active participles of weak-C_3 verbs and their verbal nouns in Forms V and VI follow this pattern.)

If the vowel before the /y/ is /a/, the simplification is even
more drastic. From the root hdy we get the theoretical forms:
*lhudayu, *lhudayi, *lhudaya → /lhudā/ 'the (right) guidance',

10

and the indefinite is, for all cases, /hudan/ '(right) guidance'.
(Note that all passive participles of derived weak-C_3 verbs, as
well as the commonest nouns of time and place derived from such
roots, follow this pattern.)

Arabic also has a narrowly defined group of nouns which differ from the above in that in the indefinite they do not take
nunation and in the genitive take short /a/, making the genitive
identical with the accusative. These words, traditionally called
diptotes, include: many proper nouns, including those of foreign
origin; plurals with the pattern $C_1aC_2\bar{a}C_3i/\bar{I}C_4$; plurals and other
grammatically feminine nouns ending with /-ā?/ where the glottal
stop does not represent a root consonant; comparatives and superlatives; and some other adjective types, as well as a number of
minor classes and special cases. The indefinite declined forms
of all these are subject to the same simplifications in the case
of weak roots; the only surprising feature is the nunation of the
nominative/genitive of diptotes with the same weakness as /qāḍī/
(see above), e.g. the theoretical form *mawāšiy- has /mawāsin/
for the nominative and genitive, with the expected /mawāšiya/
'cattle' in the accusative. All totally indeclinable nouns are
treated as are the diptotes ending in /-ay-/, i.e. they show no
case distinctions at all: /rādiyū/ 'radio'.

Dual suffixes and the 'sound' plural suffixes, which may be
used with a limited number of nouns (see below), do not differentiate the genitive and accusative: the so-called 'sound feminine plural' /-āt-/ takes nunation: nom. /lmalikātu/ 'the queens',
/malikātun/ 'queens'; gen.-accus. /lmalikāti/, /malikātin/. The
dual ending and the 'sound masculine plural' have endings which,
especially for the masculine, are reminiscent of singular case
endings, although lengthened. From the word /muslim/ 'Muslim,
one who submits', we get for the plural: nom. /muslimūna/
'Muslims'; gen.-accus. /muslimīna/; and for the dual: nom.
/muslimāni/ 'two Muslims', gen.-accus. /muslimayni/. The final
/n/ + short vowel remains when the noun is determined by the
definite article: /lmuslimūna/ 'the Muslims'; but drops when the

11

noun is followed by a determining complement: /muslimū baġdād/
'the Muslims of Baghdad'.

1.312 Gender

Gender and number are obligatory categories in both the verb and
the noun systems of Arabic.

Grammatically feminine nouns are modified by feminine adjectives and act as the subject of feminine verbs. Many grammatically feminine nouns are feminine in form, and have the feminine
ending /-at-/, which is followed by the case ending: /kalimatun/
'a word' (nom. indef.); pause form: /kalimah/. Two other endings
appear as the feminine of certain derived forms: /-āʔ-/: /ṣṣaḥrāʔu/
'the desert'; and /-ā/: /ddunyā/ 'the world'; both are diptotes.
A small number of formally feminine nouns are grammatically masculine: /xalīfah/ 'caliph'. Many nouns which are not formally feminine are so grammatically: certain paired parts of the body:
/yad/ 'hand'; names of countries, cities, and winds; /ʔarḍ/
'earth'; states of being which are explicitly female (but not all
of these): /ɛāqir/ 'barren woman'; and, above all, all plurals
which do not refer to rational beings.

The use of masculine and feminine plural forms for verbs and
modifiers is limited to nouns referring to rational beings.

1.313 Number

Number lies midway between purely inflectional processes and an
exploitation of the root and pattern system that verges on the
derivational. All duals, indicating a pair or two or any object, are formed by a suffix, and there are suffixes for masculine
and feminine plurals—the so-called 'sound' plurals (see 1.311 for
their case endings). These suffixes have initial vowels, and follow the last root consonant of the noun, except for the dual suffix, which follows the feminine ending if it is present.

	Nom. context forms	Nom. pause forms
Dual masculine	}-ā(ni)	/baytān/ 'two houses'
Dual feminine		/malikatān/ 'two queens'
Sound masc. plural	-ū(na)	/muslimūn/ 'Muslims'
Sound fem. plural	-āt(un)	/malikāt/ 'queens'

12

The sound masculine plural is used primarily with participles
of derived forms of the verb and with adjectives ending in
/-ī(y)/: /sūrīyūn/ 'Syrians'. The sound feminine plural is used
for the feminines of both the above; for many but not all words
with feminine endings in the singular, especially for those which
have corresponding masculine forms: /malikah/ 'queen' pl. /malikāt/
(compare /malik/ 'king')—this is true whether the feminine ending
has been added to indicate feminine gender or for some other derivational reason; for some masculine nouns: /ḥammām/ 'bath' pl.
/ḥammāmāt/—including many foreign ones; and for some feminines
which lack the feminine ending in the singular. For simple bases
of the form $C_1vC_2C_3$(ah), if the short vowel is /u/ or /a/, it is
often reproduced after C_2 in forming sound plurals: /ɛurs/ 'mar-
riage' pl. /ɛurusāt/, /ʔarḍ/ 'earth' pl. /ʔaraḍūn/. This is
obligatory only where v=/a/.

The vast majority of Arabic nouns have 'broken' plurals. In
these, the root consonants of the noun are rearranged with new
vowels, consonantal elements may be supplied, and feminine endings are lost. There are some thirty possible patterns for broken plurals. Only a few of them are predictable from the singular, and many are also used with other roots to form singular
nouns. Some of the most common broken plurals for words with
three consonants are the following:

$ʔaC_1C_2āC_3$	/maṯal/ 'simile, likeness' pl. /ʔamṯāl/
	/sūq/ 'market' pl. /ʔaswāq/
$C_1uC_2ūC_3$	/dars/ 'study, lesson' pl. /durūs/
	/bayt/ 'house' pl. /buyūt/
$C_1iC_2āC_3$	/rajul/ 'man' pl. /rijāl/
$C_1uC_2uC_3$	/kitāb/ 'book' pl. /kutub/
$ʔaC_1C_2uC_3$	/nahr/ 'river' pl. /ʔanhur/
$C_1uC_2C_3ān$	/balad/ 'town, country' pl. /buldān/

The first and fifth of these belong to the group of plurals traditionally called 'plurals of paucity', referring to fewer than
ten, but this distinction only holds when another plural is in
use. Many nouns have several plurals, sometimes with different

meanings: /bayt/ 'house' has a second meaning 'verse', with the plural /ʔabyāt/.

While there are recurrent relationships between the form and meaning of the singular and the form of the plural, these are not usually sufficient for prediction. However, many nouns with either a long vowel, or four consonants, or both, fall into a somewhat regular pattern, as follows:

Singular	Plural
C̄vCvC(ah)	CawāCiC (non rational)
	/ɛāmil/ 'factor', pl. /ɛawāmil/
	CuCCāC (rational)
	/ɛāmil/ 'laborer', pl. /ɛummāl/
CvC̄vC(ah)	CaCāʔiC (non-rational)
	/qasīmah/ 'coupon', pl. /qasāʔim/
	CuCaCāʔ, ʔaCCiCāʔ (rational)
	/qasīm/ 'partner', pl. /qusamāʔ/,
	/ʔaqsimāʔ/
CvCCvC(ah)	CaCāCiC (non-rational)
	/maktab/ 'office', /maktabah/ 'library'
	pl. of both /makātib/
	CaCāCiC CaCāCiCah (rational)
	/qayṣar/ 'caesar', pl. /qayāṣir/,
	/qayāṣirah/
CvCCv̄C(ah)	CaCāCĪC (non-rational)
	/maktūb/ 'letter', pl. (makātib/
	CaCāCĪC, CaCāCiCah (rational)
	/tilmīd̲/ 'pupil', pl. /talāmīd̲/,
	/talāmid̲ah/

Most of these forms can be described by the formula $C_1aC_2\bar{a}C_3i/\bar{i}C_4(ah)$, all of whose variants are diptotes except those with the feminine ending, which are in general the plurals of nouns referring to rational beings. Many of the types of singulars listed above have other possible plurals, but only those that seem to be-

long to this cluster of forms have been listed. Note that the /ī/
appears to lengthen some plurals corresponding to the bulkier singulars. Where there are fewer than four consonants in the singular,
an additional consonant is supplied in the plural: for nouns with a
long vowel in the first syllable: C_2=/w/; for nouns with a long vowel
in the second syllable: C_3=/ʔ/. The presence of a feminine ending
on the singular of nouns referring to rational beings has very little
effect on the choice of plural.

Plurals belonging to this group are also sometimes used for nouns
with more than four consonants, in which case one is usually dropped:
/ɛankabūt/ 'spider' pl. /ɛanākib/.

The broken plurals are closely related to a rather vaguely defined group of words from which they may have developed, the collectives, which act rather like such English words as 'rice' or
'fruit'. Many originally collective nouns may have been assimilated either to the singular or the plural. The collectives
which survive usually have a singular 'noun of unity', formed by
adding a feminine ending, as well as a true plural: /tuffāḥ/
'apples (col.)' resembles many such nouns (especially ones referring to plants and animals) in having a form /tuffāḥah/ 'one,
single apple' with the plural /tuffāḥāt/ 'a number of single
apples'. Another type of collective is formed by adding the feminine to adjectives: /lmuslimah/ 'the Muslims (col.)'.

1.32 Noun derivation

Except for the broken plurals, most of the previous discussion
concerns the inflection of already formed noun bases, such as
/malik/ 'king'. Such bases are, however, the result of the interlocking of at least two elements (see 1.1); in this example, the
root mlk, with the vaguely defined meaning of dominion, and the
pattern $C_1aC_2iC_3$, whose meaning and function may or may not be
definable. Because patterns vary in their specificity, it is most
efficient to approach them first formally.

1.321 Noun derivation by shifting vowel patterns

It has been demonstrated[3] that below the pattern of specific meanings for specific patterns, the possible patterns of Arabic nouns

may be analyzed in terms of a range from the briefest possible
forms the phonology allows: $C_1vC_2C_3$, augmented to $C_1vC_2vC_3$, and
further augmented by lengthening either vowels or consonants
(C_2 or C_3), with a tendency towards having the second syllable
at least as long as the first, and with a preference for doubling
C_2 to lengthen the first syllable rather than lengthening the
first vowel. The assignment of specific meanings to specific
patterns, often by the operation of analogy over long periods, is
complemented by the tendency to use the bulkier forms as more emphatic or expressive (note that plurals are, in most cases, bulkier than their singulars). Table 2 shows the range of singular
noun forms produced only by changes in patterns without affixation.
The figures after the forms indicate by the number of digits the
number of steps of increased derivational complexity. Where one
form has 'given rise' to several bulkier forms, these are identified such that CuCC ⟨3⟩ 'gives rise' to ⟨31⟩ and ⟨32⟩, while ⟨31⟩
has in turn 'produced' ⟨311⟩ and ⟨312⟩; and ⟨32⟩, similarly, has
⟨321⟩, ⟨322⟩, ⟨323⟩ and ⟨324⟩—four derived forms, some of which
have developed even further.

Arabic nouns appear with all of these shapes, with increasing
specificity as we examine the bulkier forms. Among the simpler
forms (the left-hand column) appear many primitive nouns as well
as many nouns whose use is directly related to the first (underived) form of the verb. The following forms (many with the feminine ending) are used as verbal nouns, referring simply to the
action of the verb:

⟨1⟩ ⟨11⟩ ⟨111⟩   ⟨2⟩   ⟨211⟩   ⟨3⟩   ⟨311⟩
     ⟨12⟩ ⟨122⟩   ⟨22⟩ ⟨221⟩   ·⟨32⟩ ⟨321⟩
                                                              ⟨323⟩

The feminines of ⟨1⟩ and ⟨2⟩ have specific meanings: CaCCah, the
doing of the action once; CiCCah, the manner of doing it. The
form CāCiC ⟨121⟩, e.g. /kātib/ 'writer, scribe, writing', is the
normal, productive active participle of the first form verb, but
a number of other forms designate agents, although these are not

16

Table 2

Range of Singular Noun Forms Produced by Changes in Patterns

CaCC ⟨1⟩	CaCaC ⟨11⟩	CāCaC ⟨111⟩	
		CaCāC ⟨112⟩	CaC₂C₂āC ⟨1121⟩
		CaC₂C₂aC ⟨113⟩	
		CaCaC₃C₃ ⟨114⟩	
	CaCiC ⟨12⟩	CāCiC ⟨121⟩	
		CaCīC ⟨122⟩	CiCCīC ⟨1221⟩
	CaCuC ⟨13⟩	CaCūC ⟨131⟩	CaCCūC ⟨1311⟩
			CāCūC ⟨1312⟩
		CaCuCC ⟨132⟩	
CiCC ⟨2⟩	CiCiC ⟨21⟩	CiCiCC ⟨211⟩	
	CiCaC ⟨22⟩	CiCāC ⟨221⟩	CiCCāC ⟨2211⟩
		CiCCaC ⟨222⟩	
		CiCaCC ⟨223⟩	
CuCC ⟨3⟩	CuCuC ⟨31⟩	CuCūC ⟨311⟩	
		CuCuCC ⟨312⟩	
	CuCaC ⟨32⟩	CuCāC ⟨321⟩	CuCCāC ⟨3221⟩
		CuCCaC ⟨322⟩	
		CuCaCC ⟨323⟩	
		CuCayC ⟨324⟩	CuCCayC ⟨3241⟩

generally productive:

⟨1⟩ ⟨11⟩ ⟨112⟩   ⟨2⟩   ⟨3⟩ ⟨31⟩
      ⟨12⟩ ⟨121⟩   ⟨32⟩ ⟨321⟩
              ⟨122⟩
      ⟨13⟩ ⟨131⟩

Of these, CaCīC ⟨122⟩ and CaCūC ⟨131⟩ are associated with con-
tinual or habitual action. The first is especially common, pro-
ducing large classes of familiar nouns: /ṭawīl/ 'long, tall
(being long)', /ṣadīq/ 'friend (being true, reliable)'. Moving
from these further to the right, we find a whole series of intensive forms: ⟨1121⟩ ⟨1311⟩ ⟨1312⟩ ⟨2211⟩ ⟨322⟩ ⟨3221⟩: /širrīb/

'drunkard', /sabbūḥ/ 'all pure, all glorious', etc. CaCCāC ⟨1121⟩
has acquired, by analogy with Aramaic borrowings, the specific use
of the name of a profession: /xayyāṭ/ 'tailor', /najjār/ 'carpen-
ter'; the same form with the feminine ending added is used for the
instrument of habitual activity: the /ṭayyār/ 'aviator' flies a
/ṭayyārah/, whereas for the other intensives the feminine ending
is more likely to denote increased intensity.

Among the columns on the right-hand side of the chart, the particular semantic content of a root gives to the simple idea of intensity a number of connotations: pejorative, diminutive, or aug-
mentative. In addition, Arabic has a set form for the diminutive:
CuCayC ⟨324⟩, e.g. /kalb/ 'dog' /kulayb/ 'little dog', which can
be used quite freely. Other partially standardized uses of patterns are CiCāC ⟨221⟩ for a container or tool: /jirāb/ 'bag';
CuCāC ⟨321⟩ for a disease; /suɛāl/ 'cough'; CiCāCah for a function
or office; /wizārah/ 'ministry'. It is also worth noting the
large number of these patterns (with a preference for the third
group, containing /u/ in the first syllable) that are used for
broken plurals or collectives:

$$⟨11⟩ \qquad ⟨2⟩ \quad ⟨22⟩ \quad ⟨221⟩ \qquad ⟨3⟩ \quad ⟨31⟩ \quad ⟨311⟩$$
$$⟨32⟩ \qquad\qquad ⟨3212⟩$$
$$⟨322⟩$$

1.322 Noun derivation by affixation

A further group of Arabic noun patterns involves affixes containing
the consonants /m t n y ?/. Many of these are specifically related
to verbs; only those related to simple verbs will be discussed here,
while nouns related to derived verbs will be discussed later.

(a) Prefix /m-/

    (1) maC_1C_2i/aC_3(ah) indicates either the time or the place
of an action: /maktab/ 'office', /maktabah/ 'library',
(/kátab/ 'write'); /majlis/ 'session' (/jalas/ 'sit');
/mawɛid/ 'time or place of rendezvous' (/waɛad/
'promise'). The vowel of C_2 is /a/ unless the imperfect
stem of the verb has /i/. Many of these forms are simply
verbal nouns: /maɛrifah/ 'knowledge'.

18

(2) $miC_1C_2aC_3(ah)$ or $miC_1C_2\bar{a}C_3$ indicate an instrument:
/miftāḥ/ 'key, opener' (/fataḥ/ 'open'); these forms,
along with a form with /ī/ in the second syllable,
appear as intensive adjectives in a few frozen forms,
although the pattern is not productive: /miskīn/ 'poor,
wretched'.

(3) $maC_1C_2\bar{u}C_3$ is the passive participle of the simple form
of the verb: /maktūb/ 'that which is written, letter'.
The /m/ prefix is used throughout the system of derived
verbs for participles, nouns of time and place, and
auxiliary verbal nouns, but the vowel system is less
flexible and the forms are not as clearly differentiated.

(b) <u>Prefix</u> /t-/

The form $taC_1C_2v/\bar{v}C_3$ is quite common, but there is no specific
association of meaning with nouns with the prefix /ta-/ except
as verbal nouns of some derived verbs. Otherwise, these forms
appear intermittently as verbal nouns, sometimes being trans-
ferred to the agent of the action as intensive adjectives.

(c) <u>Prefix</u> /ʔ-/

Outside of the system of derived verbs, the prefixed glottal
stop has three principal uses: (a) in forming several different
plurals, especially the 'plurals of paucity'; (b) for the com-
parative-superlative $ʔaC_1C_2aC_3$, which has the feminine $C_1uC_2 \cdot$
$C_3\bar{a}$: /ʔaḥsanu rajulin/ 'the fairest of men', /lmalikatu
ljumlā/ 'the most beautiful queen'; both diptotes; (c) for
adjectives denoting colors or physical peculiarities, with
the form $ʔaC_1C_2aC_3$ in the masculine and $C_1aC_2C_3\bar{a}ʔ$ in the feminine; both diptotes: /ʔaḥdab/ 'hunchbacked (masc. sing.)';
/ʔaṣamm/ (← *ʔaṣmam, root ṣmm) 'deaf (masc. sing.)'; /ḥamrāʔ/
'red (fem. sing.)'.

(d) <u>Suffix</u> /-ā/

$C_1aC_2C_3\bar{a}$ is the plural of a number of adjectives of various
forms indicating injuries or defects: /marīḍ/ 'sick' pl.
/marḍā/: and the feminine of adjectives with suffixed /-ān/:
/kaslān/ 'lazy' fem. /kaslā/. (See above for $C_1uC_2C_3\bar{a}$ as the

feminine of $?aC_1C_2aC_3$.) $C_1vC_2C_3\bar{a}$ produces a number of verbal nouns: /daεw$\bar{a}$/ from /da$\varepsilon\bar{a}$/ 'call', root dεw; /dikr$\bar{a}$/ from /dakar/ 'remember, mention'.

(e) Suffix /-$\bar{a}$?/

This is an inflectional form, yielding the feminine of adjectives for colors and physical peculiarities (see above), and two plurals, both used for nouns denoting rational beings: /waz$\bar{i}$r/ 'minister' pl. /wuzar$\bar{a}$?/, /qar$\bar{i}$b/ 'relative' pl. /?aqrib$\bar{a}$?/.

(f) Suffix /-$\bar{a}$n/

$C_1i/uC_2C_3\bar{a}$n is a plural: /?ixw$\bar{a}$n/ 'brothers', /furs$\bar{a}$n/ 'horsemen'. $C_1a/uC_2C_3\bar{a}$n (with /a/, sometimes a diptote) refers to the agent of the verb: /nadm$\bar{a}$n/ 'penitent'. $C_1i/uC_2C_3\bar{a}$n or $C_1aC_2aC_3\bar{a}$n are verbal nouns: /šukr$\bar{a}$n/ 'thanks', /hayaj$\bar{a}$n/ 'agitation'.

(g) Suffix /-$\bar{i}$y-/

This suffix is added to nouns, especially loanwords, to form relative adjectives which may be used as nouns: /miṣr/ 'Egypt' /miṣr$\bar{i}$y/ 'Egyptian, an Egyptian'. When the feminine ending is added, a feminine ('an Egyptian woman'), a collective, or an abstract noun is produced: /qawm/ 'nation', /qawm$\bar{i}$y/ 'national', /qawm$\bar{i}$yah/ 'nationalism'. This is an extremely productive form, for although the classical grammarians defined a number of complex rules for affixing /-$\bar{i}$y/, modern Arab writers ignore many of them, so that, in effect, this suffix can be used with virtually no attention to the internal structure of the word.

(h) Feminine ending

The feminine suffix /-at-/ has been mentioned in a wide variety of contexts, and only its major uses will be reiterated here.

Most noun forms which can refer to female beings, particularly the verbal adjectives, can receive this suffix (note that the other types of feminines are limited to specific derivational patterns); most forms of verbal nouns occur with

the feminine ending, sometimes with the specification of doing the action once; and most collectives are made singular
by adding it. Intensive adjectives are made more intensive
by the feminine, and it occurs in a number of plurals, especially those referring to rational beings, or containing
semivowels in the root.

1.33 The Arabic number system

The Arabs use a system of numbers that work on the same principle as those that we call Arabic, but with different orthographic
forms: they are called Indian by the Arabs, after the earlier borrowing, and are written in the same decimal order (from left to right)
as our own. The inflection of these numbers—formed on ancient
roots which are limited to this subsection of the morphology—and
of nouns accompanying them, is handled gingerly, if at all, even
by highly educated Arabs.

'One' /wāhid/, fem. /wāhidah/, and 'two' /tnān/, fem. /tnatān/,
are excepted from the general number system; they are adjectives
and follow the noun, agreeing with it in gender, number (/tnān/
is a dual form), definiteness, and case; 3-10 also have masculine
and feminine forms, working on a principle which is apparently
the opposite of that used for nouns: /sabɛah/ 'seven (masc.)',
/sabɛ/ 'seven (fem.)'; 11-19 retain this gender for the digits,
followed by a special form of the noun 'ten' whose apparent gender agrees with that of the noun: /ɛašarah/ 'ten (masc.)', /ɛašr/
'ten (fem.)'; /ɛašar/ '-teen (masc.)', /ɛašrah/ '-teen (fem.)'.
These numbers, i.e. 11-19, are undeclinable, being supplied with
final /-(t)a/: /sabɛata ɛašara/ 'seventeen (masc.)'; 20 has the
unexpected form /ɛisrūn/, but all the other multiples of ten are
simply the sound masculine plurals of the digits, e.g. /sabɛūn/
'seventy', with no gender difference. The words for a hundred,
/miʔah/ (no plural in this context) and a thousand, /ʔalf/ (pl.
/ʔālāf/) are treated like normal nouns, one masculine and the
other feminine; they can be multiplied ('seven hundreds'), or
appear in the singular or the dual.

The major difficulty with the numbers is syntactic, and becomes very complex when they are compounded, depending on the role of the object being enumerated in the sentence. In compound numbers, each form is linked to the following one by the conjunction /wa-/ 'and', e.g. /miʔatun wa-sabɛūna/ '170', except the two portions of the numbers between 11 and 19. These forms, and the forms for 21-99 (excluding simple multiples of ten), are cited in the reverse order of magnitude: the 'tens' following the 'units', e.g. 'seventeen', 'seven and seventy'. The case and number of the noun are determined by the last number form in the series: the relationship is either a special frozen syntactic pattern (noun in accusative singular) or the normal relationship between a noun (here a number), which has the case appropriate to its position in the sentence, and a following determining complement (the noun enumerated) in the genitive (see 1.73). Number forms which take immediately following nouns as determining complements, e.g. /ʔarbaɛatu rijālin/ 'four men', become indefinite when another digit follows, establishing its own relationship with the noun, e.g. /ʔarbaɛatun wa-ʔarbaɛūna rajulan/ 'four and forty men'.

The forms of the noun are as follows:

	Last number form:
Accusative singular	13-99 (incl.)
Genitive	
(determining complement following number with sentence case)	
(a) Singular	100, 1000
	(+ round multiples of either)
(b) Plural	3-10

Examples (with full context forms): /sabɛatu mulūkin/ '7 kings', /sabɛu malikātin/ '7 queens'; /sabɛata ɛašara malikan/ '17 kings', /sabɛa ɛašrata malikatan/ '17 queens'; /sabɛatun wa-sabɛūna malikan/ '77 kings', /sabɛun wa-sabɛūna malikatan/ '77 queens'; /sabɛatu ʔālāfin wa-sabɛu miʔatin wa-sabɛatun wa-sabɛūna malikan/ '7,777 kings'; /qabla miʔatayni wa-sabɛīna malikan/ 'before 270

22

kings'; /ʔalfā malikatin wa-malikatun (wāḥidatun)/ '2,001 queens'.

For long numbers, especially dates, the order may be: digits, tens, hundreds, thousands. Note that this order corresponds with the fact that the written ciphers follow a left to right sequence.

The roots that form the digits are used for the final digit of ordinals, in the form of active participles: /sābiɛ/ 'seventh (masc.)'; and for fractions, distributive numbers, etc.: /subɛ/ or /subuɛ/ 'one seventh', /subāɛīy/ 'consisting of seven parts, seven by seven', /sabbaɛ/ 'he made sevenfold, divided in seven parts', etc.

1.4 The verb

Arabic has a rich and flexible verb system which is far more regular and predictable than the noun system. Person, aspect, and mode are indicated primarily by affixes; internal patterning produces a number of derived forms which are intensive, causative, reflexive, etc., each derived form being associated with a set of participles and verbal nouns; a further system of vowel shifts differentiates active and passive verbs.

1.41 Verbal inflection

Arabic has two sets of verb forms, traditionally called perfect and imperfect. The perfect refers to past time (or completed action) and the imperfect to present or future time (and incompleted action): /katab/ 'he wrote, he has written', /yaktub/ 'he writes, he is writing, he will write'. Finer distinctions are indicated by the use of particles and auxiliary verbs. For both sets of forms, the categories of gender and number are retained, but are not fully indicated for all three persons. A partial set of duals is formed by adding /-ā/ to the masc. and fem. third person singular in both tenses, and to the masc. second person singular (in the imperfect) and plural (in the perfect), or, if this creates an impossible form, to the reconstructed form on which these persons are based. The perfect indicates all categories by means of suffixes, while the imperfect makes a partially realized distinction between the use of prefixes, for

person, and suffixes, similar to the nominal suffixes, for gender
and number. The imperfect has a further set of endings indicating
mode (which does not occur with perfect verbs) and is used without prefixes for the imperative.

1.411 Person, gender, and number

The person, gender, and number affixes of the verb are shown in
Table 3. Simple, underived verbs have the perfect base $C_1aC_2vC_3$-:

Table 3

Person, Number, and Gender Affixes of the Verb

Perfect			Imperfect
3rd person			
masc. sing.	/-a/		/ya/u-/
fem. sing.	/-at/		/ta/u-/
masc. pl.	/-ū/		/ya/u--ū-/
fem. pl.	/-na/		/ya/u--na/
masc. dual	/-ā/		/ya/u--ā-/
fem. dual	/-atā/		/ta/u--ā-/
2nd person			
masc. sing.	/-ta/		/ta/u-/
fem. sing.	/-ti/		/ta/u--ī-/
masc. pl.	/-tum/		/ta/u--ū-/
fem. pl.	/-tunna/		/ta/u--na/
dual	/-tumā/		/ta/u--ā-/
1st person			
sing.	/tu/		/ʔa/u-/
pl.	/-nā/		/na/u-/

/šaribtum/ 'you (masc. pl.) drank'. The third person sing. masc.
is the standard dictionary form: /kataba/ 'he wrote', often
glossed simply 'write'. The imperfect base is -$C_1C_2vC_3$-, with
/a/ in the prefix: /yaktub-/, /tašrabū-/, etc.

In the base forms of simple verbs (see 1.421), all three short

vowels occur in both tenses. The number of possible vowels is
somewhat simplified for 'weak' verbs (containing a semivowel),
and the choice of vowels for the two aspects is more closely related.

1.412 Mode

The imperfect is called by the Arabs /lmuḍāriɛ/ 'the resembling
[form]' because the three modes are said to resemble the cases
of the noun. They are traditionally called the indicative, the
subjunctive, and the jussive (a case with a very limited use related to the imperative); they have the following endings:

	After -C₃	After -v̄	After -v
Indicative	-u	-na (fem. & pl.)	zero
		-ni (dual)	
Subjunctive	-a	zero	zero
Jussive (Imperative)	zero/-(i)	zero	zero

The similarity to the noun system is based on the fact that the
jussive, when it ends in a consonant, may be supplied with /i/
to resolve a following consonant cluster. The positive imperative is simply the second person form of the jussive stripped of
prefixes, with the resulting cluster (if any) resolved (see 1.23):
/ʔuktub/ 'write! (masc. sing.)', /ʔišrabna/ 'drink! (fem. pl.)'.
Examples: indic. /yaktubu/ 'he writes', subj. /yaktuba/ 'that he
write'; indic. /yašrabāni/ 'they two (masc.) drink', subj.
/yašrabā/ 'that they two (masc.) drink'.

A further set of suffixes, called 'energetic', may be added
to the jussive or imperative: /-(a)n(na/i)/: /yaktuban/,
yaktubanna/ third person masc. sing. These forms are complicated
and are rarely used.

1.413 Roots with C₁ = /ʔ/ or Y̶

Roots with initial /ʔ/ are simplified according to the rule that
*ʔvʔ- becomes /ʔv̄-/: /ʔākulu/ ← *ʔaʔkulu 'I eat'; the initial /ʔ/
is often lost in the imperative: /kul/ 'eat'. In other parts of
the root, the glottal stop behaves regularly (though it presents
some difficulty in learning Arabic because there are different
ways of writing it).

C_1 = /w/ drops in the primary form of high frequency roots between /a/ and C_2: /yajidu/ 'he finds' ← *yawjidu, root wjd. Elsewhere, the resulting possible combinations for initial weak verbs retain the short vowel and semivowel before long vowels, but reduce them to possible long vowels or diphthongs before consonants, the semivowel assimilating to the vowel. C_1 = /w/ assimilates to an infixed /t/ (see 1.422).

1.414 <u>Roots with</u> C_2 = Ɏ or C_3

C_2 = /y/ has one possible set of bases: $C_1 ayiC_3$- and -$C_1 yiC_3$-; C_2 = /w/ has two possible sets of bases: $C_1 awuC_3$-/-$C_1 wuC_3$- and $C_1 awiC_3$-/-$C_1 waC_3$-. In their inflection and derivation, clusters of vowels and semivowels are formed, which are simplified as follows: (a) /i/, /u/ of C_1 + Ɏ + $vC_3 \rightarrow \bar{v}C_3$; (b) /a/ + Ɏ + $vC_3 \rightarrow$ /$\bar{a}C_3$/, except in the primary verb in those persons of the perfect which have suffixes beginning with a consonant (i.e. in closed syllables), which follow rule (a); (c) a semivowel that is doubled or preceded by a long vowel retains its form, except in the active participle of primary verbs (*$q\bar{a}wim \rightarrow$ /$q\bar{a}ʔim$/ 'standing') and in verbal nouns (/i/ + Ɏ + $\bar{a}C_3 \rightarrow iy\bar{a}C_3$; C + Ɏ + $\bar{a}C_3 \rightarrow C\bar{a}C_3$). As always, where these processes produce long vowels in closed syllables, the vowel is shortened. Examples of the three types (in order): /$yab\bar{i}\varepsilon u$/ 'he buys' (indic.), /$yabi\varepsilon$/ (juss.), /$b\bar{a}\varepsilon a$/ 'he bought'—but /$bi\varepsilon tu$/ 'I bought'; /yaqumu/ 'he gets up', /yaqum/, /$q\bar{a}ma$/, /qumtu/; /$yan\bar{a}mu$/ 'he sleeps', /yanam/, /$n\bar{a}ma$/, /nimtu/.

Where two identical last consonants of a root (i.e. C_2 = C_3) are separated by a short vowel, as -$C_2 vC_3$, they are rearranged wherever the surrounding syllable structure will permit, as -$(v)C_2 C_3$- throughout the verb system and in nouns directly derived from verbs (e.g. not in plurals: /judud/, 'new (pl.)'); in participles: /ḍall/ ← *ḍ$\bar{a}$lil (the commonest source of overlong syllables); nouns of place: /maḥall/ 'place' ← *maḥlal; comparatives: /ʔahamm/ 'more important' ← *ʔahmam, etc. This results in the following verb forms: /radda/ 'he returned'—but /radadta/ 'you (masc. sing.) returned'; /yaruddu/ 'he returns'

(indic.)—but, in the jussive, /yardud/. Note that since the
same factors of syllable structure are operating, the same persons that have /v̄/ if C_2 = ꙟ, have a doubled consonant if C_2 =
C_3: /yaqūmu/, /yaruddu/; while those which have a short vowel
separate the consonants: /qumta/, /radadta/.

1.415 <u>Roots with</u> C_3 = ꙟ

C_3 = /w/ has one principle set of bases: C_1aC_2aw-/-C_1C_2uw-;
C_3 = /y/ has two: C_1aC_2ay-/-C_1C_2iy and C_1aC_2iy-/-C_1C_2ay-. These
bases are handled as follows:

(a) for any suffix beginning with a long vowel, the corresponding
semivowel replaces C_3, and the short vowel of the suffix is
lost:

mašay- + -ū (= -uw) → /mašaw/ 'they (masc.) walked': $\begin{array}{l}ay\text{-}\\ \text{-}uw\end{array}$;

tadεuw- + -īna (= -iyna) → *tadεuyna → /tadεīna/ 'you
(fem. sing.) call': $\begin{array}{l}uw\text{-}\\ \text{-}iy\end{array}$;

(b) phonologically excluded vowel-semivowel clusters, i.e. all
but the long /ī/ and /ū/, which may be followed by /a/ or
/ā/ (iyǎ, uwǎ), and the diphthongs, which may be followed by
/ā/, are simplified and reduced by the assimilation of a preceding /i/ or /u/ (and any vowels following the cluster) to
the semivowel (→ /ī/ or /ū/), or of the semivowel to preceding /a/:

/tadεuwa/ 'that you (masc. sing.) call' (subj.);

/taεawta/ 'you (masc. sing.) called';

/tamšī/ 'you (masc. sing.) walk' ← *tamšiyu;—but /mašā/
'he walked' ← *mašaya;

(c) when the result in the jussive is a final long vowel that
does not indicate gender or number, it is shortened:

	indic.	subj.	juss.
you (masc. sing.)	/tadεū/	/tadεuwa/	/tadεu/
you (fem. sing.)	/tadεīna/	/tadεī/	/tadεī/

(d) further changes may of course be required by the syllable
structure:

/mašat/ 'she walked' ← *mašāt ← *mašayat.

Complex as these rules are, they are applied with great regularity, although they result in the loss of a number of distinctions, e.g. /yadɛūna/, 'they call' results from both *yadɛuwūna (masc. pl. imperf.) and *yadɛuwna (fem. pl. imperf.). Furthermore, the similarity of the imperfect verb and the noun comes in surprisingly handy here: the final syllables of those persons of the imperfect for C_3 = /y/ which do not have suffixes for gender and number correspond closely to the case endings of definite nouns with final C_3 = /y/. For the derived verbs, the vowel preceding C_3 is part of an invariable pattern (always /a/ or /i/) and C_3 = Y̦ is always treated as /y/, so that the relationship between the final syllable and the suffixes may be handled without any reference to changes earlier in the word. Like C_2 = Y̦, C_3 = Y̦ becomes /ʔ/ after /ā/ (i.e. in the verbal nouns of derived verbs). Table 4 should clarify the application of these rules (only part of the conjugation is shown, from which the remainder may easily be inferred).

1.42 Verbal derivation

As in the case of the nouns, Arabic verbs show a progressive movement from the simple form, containing only the three root consonants and short vowels, which has been considered thus far, to much more complex forms produced by lengthening vowels or consonants or by adding consonantal elements. However, the verb system differs from the noun system in that after the first derivational step beyond the primary verbs, which have a number of possible vowel patterns, each derived form appears with only one possible vowel pattern. However, the vowel patterns of both primary and derived verbs may give way to an additional pattern, that of the passive, which is constant throughout.

1.421 The formation of primary verbs

Primary verbs in Arabic have the stem $C_1aC_2vC_3$- in the perfect, and -$C_1C_2vC_3$- in the imperfect. They always have /a/ in the first syllable of the perfect, and in the imperfect they use prefixes containing /a/. The variable short vowels of primary verbs—marked by the symbol (v)—must be lexically specified in each case.

28

Table 4

Conjugation of Verbs with Roots with C_3 = Y̌

děw 'call'		m̌sy 'walk'		bqy 'remain'	
Perfect	C_1aC_2aw-	Perfect	C_1aC_2ay-	Perfect	C_1aC_2iy-
3 m.s.	/daɛā/	/masǎā/		/baqiya/	
3 f.s.	/daɛat/	/masǎat/		/baqiyat/	
3 m.pl.	/daɛaw/	/masǎaw/		/baqū/	
3 f.pl.	/daɛawna/	/masǎayna/		/baqīna/	
3 m.d.	/daɛawā/	/masǎayā/		/baqiyā/	
3 f.d.	/daɛatā/	/masǎatā/		/baqiyatā/	
2 m.s.	/daɛawta/	/masǎayta/		/baqīta/	
Imperf.	$-C_1C_2uw-$	Imperf.	$-C_1C_2iy-$	Imperf.	$-C_1C_2ay-$
Indic.					
2 m.s.	/tadɛū/	/tamšī/		/tabqā/	
2 f.s.	/tadɛīna/	/tamšīna/		/tabqayna/	
2 m.pl.	/tadɛūna/	/tamšūna/		/tabqawna/	
2 f.pl.	/tadɛūna/	/tamšīna/		/tabqayna/	
2 m.d.	/tadɛuwāni/	/tamšiyāni/		/tabqayāni/	
Jussive					
2 m.s.	/tadɛu/	/tamši/		/tabqa/	
Subjunctive					
2 m.s.	/tadɛuwa/	/tamšiya/		/tabqā/	

For the 'weak' verbs, the system is distorted, so that there are
only a few possibilities, and these may be arbitrarily specified
to provide for the simplest formal statement of the behavior of
particular groups of verbs. All other verbs seem to reflect some
ancient derivational process without being perfectly regular,
since they have been disrupted by analogies and semantic shift.
Even among the verbs which do not have weak C_2 or C_3, certain
phonological conditions can interfere with the derivational pattern, but they must be described as deviations from it. The
semantic content is attached primarily to the vowel of the perfect,

which is only a partial basis for predicting the vowel of the
imperfect.

1. short /a/ in the perfect: $C_1aC_2aC_3-$ (usually transitive):
   (a) imperfect $-C_1C_2uC_3-$; this is the commonest form of
       primary verb: /katab yaktub/ 'write', /qatal yaqtul/
       'kill, murder';
   (b) imperfect $-C_1C_2iC_3-$; may denote briefer or more super-
       ficial actions than the preceding form: /ḍarab yaḍrib/
       'hit';

2. short /i/ in the perfect; $C_1aC_2iC_3-$ (usually intransitive,
   often expressing a temporary state, including the holding
   of an opinion or attitude); imperfect $-C_1C_2aC_3-$: /fariḥ
   yafraḥ/ 'rejoice', /ḥasib yaḥsab/ 'think, consider';

3. short /u/ in the perfect; $C_1aC_2uC_3-$ (usually intransitive,
   expressing a permanent state or the acquisition of a lasting trait); imperfect $-C_1C_2uC_3-$: /qabuḥ yaqbuḥ/ 'be ugly',
   /ḥasun yaḥsun/ 'be beautiful'.

The principal phonological factors disrupting this are (a) the
existence of an additional pattern with v=/a/ for both aspects,
which is followed only by verbs with C_2 or C_3 = a back consonant,
i.e. /g̊ x ɛ ḥ ʔ h/: /baɛaṯ yabɛaṯ/ 'send'; (b) if C_1 = /w/, verbs
of type 1(a) have /i/ in the imperfect: /wajad yajid/ 'find'; and
verbs of type 1(b) have /i/ in the perfect as well: /wariṯ yariṯ/
'inherit'.

A further factor of asymmetry is the increased tendency to use
prepositions with verbs of motion which were originally transitive and have transitive vowel patterns. However, the distinctions do have some reality: /ḥazan yaḥzun/ 'sadden' vs. /ḥazin
yaḥzan/ 'be sad, grieve'; /kabar yakbur/ 'exceed (someone) in
age' vs. /kabur yakbur/ 'become great'; /safil yasfal/ 'be low'
vs. /saful yasful/ 'be base, despicable'.

1.422 Derived verbs

Arabic has some fourteen derived verb forms, only ten of which
will concern us here, the remainder being very rare and unproductive. In the perfect, all have /a/ or /ā/ throughout, except

where other vowels are introduced in the regular manner to resolve initial clusters. In the imperfect, each form is characterized by its first vowel, i.e. by the use of /a/ or /u/ with the
personal prefixes, and by the vowel following C_2; all other vowel
positions that occur are filled by /a/ or /ā/. The traditional
Arabic order of the forms which concern us here (Forms II - XI)
is unilluminating from the point of view of content, etymology
or syllabic structure; it is, however, designed to illuminate the
different vowel patterns of the imperfect (see Table 5).

Table 5

Vowel Patterns of the Imperfect of the Derived Verbs

u---i		a---a		a---i	
II	$yuC_1aC_2C_2iC_3-$	V	$yataC_1aC_2C_2aC_3-$	VII	$yanC_1aC_2iC_3-$
III	$yuC_1āC_2iC_3-$	VI	$yataC_1āC_2aC_3-$	VIII	$yaC_1taC_2iC_3-$
IV	$yuC_1C_2iC_3-$			IX	$*yaC_1C_2aC_3iC_3-$
				→	$yaC_1C_2aC_3C_3-$
				X	$yastaC_1C_2iC_3-$
				XI	$*yaC_1C_2āC_3iC_3-$
				→	$yaC_1C_2āC_3C_3-$

The three columns in Table 5 provide some information on other
forms of the verbs: the perfects may be formed for the second
column simply by stripping off the third person prefix of the
imperfect, while for the first and third columns, all the vowels
must be changed to /a/ and, for the third, an anaptyctic vowel
and glottal stop provided: (ʔi)nCaCaC-, (ʔi)CtaCaC-, etc. The
same base acts as verbal noun for Forms V and VI, with the change
of the vowel of C_2 to /u/; and for Forms VII-X, with the first
stem vowel changed to /i/ and the last to /ā/: $taC_1aC_2C_2uC_3$,
(ʔi)$C_1tiC_2āC_3$, (ʔi)$stiC_1C_2āC_3$, etc. The items in the first column have the following forms:

31

Perfect	Verbal noun
II $C_1aC_2C_2aC_3$-	$taC_1C_2\bar{\imath}C_3$
III $C_1\bar{a}C_2aC_3$-	$C_1iC_2\bar{a}C_3$ or $muC_1\bar{a}C_2aC_3ah$
IV $\text{?}aC_1C_2aC_3$-	$\text{?}iC_1C_2\bar{a}C_3$

A structural examination of the derived verb forms shows that four of them, Forms II, III, IX, and XI, are produced without additional consonantal elements: by lengthening a vowel, by doubling C_2, or by doubling C_3. Form IV has a prefixed /?/ in the perfect: $\text{?}aC_1C_2C_3$-; while Form VII has a prefix /n/. All of the remaining forms have a prefixed or infixed /t/, with the general effect of making the form less transitive, often reflexive or reciprocal.

more transitive	less transitive
I $C_1aC_2vC_3$-/$yaC_1C_2vC_3$-	VIII $(\text{?}i)C_1taC_2aC_3$-/$yaC_1taC_2iC_3$-
II $C_1aC_2C_2aC_3$-/$yuC_1aC_2C_2iC_3$-	V $taC_1aC_2C_2aC_3$-/$yataC_1aC_2C_2aC_3$-
III $C_1\bar{a}C_2aC_3$-/$yuC_1\bar{a}C_2iC_3$-	VI $taC_1\bar{a}C_2aC_3$-/$yataC_1\bar{a}C_2aC_3$-
IV $\text{?}aC_1C_2aC_3$-/$yuC_1C_2iC_3$-	X $(\text{?}i)staC_1C_2aC_3$-/$yastaC_1C_2iC_3$-

However, the forms have acquired other connotations, and some of the relationships are only of historical and etymological interest, e.g. the /?/ of Form IV is historically related to the /s/ of Form X.

SUMMARY OF DERIVED VERBS AND THEIR MEANINGS

The following primary verbs serve as references for overlapping examples of the relationships between simple and derived forms: /ɛalim/ 'know', /ḥasun/ 'be good, beautiful', /kaḏab/ 'lie', /katab/ 'write', /šaḡal/ 'occupy', /qatal/ 'kill'. In the summary below, prosthetic syllables are indicated in parentheses for the canonical forms but omitted in the examples.

II $C_1aC_2C_2aC_3$-, $yuC_1aC_2C_2iC_3$-, $taC_1C_2\bar{\imath}C_3$:

    (a) to do intensively or repeatedly: /qattal/ 'massacre', /šaḡḡal/ 'engross, employ';

    (b) to cause to do: /ɛallam/ 'teach';

    (c) to believe or declare something is done: /kaḏḏab/ 'accuse of lying, refute'.

III $C_1\bar{a}C_2aC_3$-, $yuC_1\bar{a}C_2iC_3$-, $muC_1\bar{a}C_2aC_3ah \sim C_1iC_2\bar{a}C_3$:

(a) to endeavor to do something: /qātal/ 'fight with and try
   to kill';

(b) to direct an action or quality toward someone: /kātab/
   'write to', /ḥasan/ 'treat kindly' (if Form I requires a
   preposition, Form III is directly transitive).

IV $ʔaC_1C_2aC_3$-, $yuC_1C_2iC_3$-, $ʔiC_1C_2āC_3$:

(a) to cause to do: /ʔaɛlam/ 'inform', /ʔaktab/ 'dictate',
   /ʔakdab/ 'cause to lie';

(b) to believe or declare something is done: /ʔakdab/ 'call
   or prove a liar';

(c) to characterize to an extraordinary degree (with /mā/;
   used in third person perf. only): /mā ʔaḥsanahu/ 'how
   handsome he is!'

V $taC_1aC_2C_2aC_3$-, $yataC_1aC_2C_2aC_3$-, $taC_1aC_2C_2uC_3$: to become, to
enter the state cause by II(b) or do it to oneself: /taɛallam/
'become learned', /taḥassan/ 'improve, become better'.

VI $taC_1āC_2aC_3$-, $yataC_1āC_2aC_3$-, $taC_1āC_2uC_3$:

(a) to pretend or simulate: /tašāgal/ 'pretend to be busy';

(b) to act mutually: /taqātal/ 'fight with each other',
   /takātab/ 'correspond'.

VII $(ʔi)nC_1aC_2aC_3$-, $yanC_1aC_2iC_3$-, $(ʔi)nC_1iC_2āC_3$: to have (or allow
to be) done to oneself: /nšagal/ 'be occupied, kept busy'.

VIII $(ʔi)C_1taC_2aC_3$-, $yaC_1taC_2iC_3$-, $(ʔi)C_1tiC_2āC_3$: reflexive of I:
/ktatab/ 'be registered, recorded; copy': /qtatal/ 'fight with
each other'.

IX $(ʔi)C_1C_2aC_3C_3$-, $yaC_1C_2aC_3C_3$-, $(ʔi)C_1C_2iC_3āC_3$: to become characterized by a particular color or physical defect: /ḥmarr/
'become red', /ɛwajj/ 'become crooked'.

X $(ʔi)staC_1C_2aC_3$-, $yastaC_1C_2iC_3$-, $(ʔi)stiC_1C_2āC_3$:

(a) to ask someone to do something: /staktab/ 'ask someone to
   write';

(b) reflexive of IV: /staɛlam/ 'inquire, seek information';

(c) to attribute a quality: /staḥsan/ 'consider good,
   admire, sanction'.

XI $(ʔi)C_1C_2āC_3C_3$-, $yaC_1C_2āC_3C_3$-, $(ʔi)C_1C_2īC_3āC_3$: a rare form
identical in meaning with IX: /ʔaswādd/ 'become black'.

Even in this idealized form, it is clear that the system is
far from rigid: Forms II and IV, IX and XI, as well as Forms VI,
VII, and VIII, show immediate possibilities of overlap; most
forms have additional specialized usages not mentioned here; and
most derivations from the primary form depend on whether the
primary form is transitive or not. Roots generally appear in
only three or four forms, but further derived forms may be coined.
Anciently coined forms have often drifted into meanings which seem
totally arbitrary or have become highly specific.

Nominal roots may be given different kinds of verbal meaning
by verbal derivation, usually in the following patterns:

II to become or be occupied with something: /šarraq/ 'go east'
   (cf. /šarq/ 'east');

IV to produce something, pretend to be something: /ʔamṭar/
   'produce rain' (cf. /maṭar/ 'rain'); /ʔaqfar/ 'become desert'
   (cf. /qafr/ 'desert');

X to ask for something: /stamṭar/ 'ask for rain'.

1.4221 Passive verbs

All of these forms, except Forms VII, IX and XI, may be put into
the passive voice, as may the first form. Passive verbs have, in
the perfect, the vowel sequence u---i, with the /i/ directly preceding C_3, and /u/ or /ū/ in all other positions in the stem:
Form I $C_1uC_2iC_3$-; Form V $tuC_1uC_2C_2iC_3$-; Form X $(ʔu)stuC_1C_2iC_3$-;
etc., and in the imperfect, by the sequence u---a, with /u/ for
the personal prefix and /a/ or /ā/ throughout the stem: Form X
$yustaC_1C_2aC_3$-.

In addition to the verbal nouns, active and passive participles may be derived from all these forms: this is most simply
schematized if passive participles are shown by substituting /m/
for the consonant of the personal prefix of the imperfect passive,
and active participles by changing the vowel before C_3 to /i/:

	Imp. Active	Imp. Passive	Pass. partic.	Act. partic.
II	$yuC_1aC_2C_2iC_3$-	$yuC_1aC_2C_2aC_3$-	$muC_1aC_2C_2aC_3$	$muC_1aC_2C_2iC_3$
V	$yataC_1aC_2C_2aC_3$-	$yutaC_1aC_2C_2aC_3$-	$mutaC_1aC_2C_2aC_3$	$mutaC_1aC_2C_2iC_3$
X	$yastaC_1C_2iC_3$-	$yustaC_1C_2aC_3$-	$mustaC_1C_2aC_3$	$mustaC_1C_2iC_3$

This is the case by analogy even if the intervening forms do not occur:

VII $yanC_1aC_2iC_3$- *$yunC_1aC_2aC_3$- *$munC_1aC_2aC_3$ $munC_1aC_2iC_3$

In the derived systems, the multitude of nouns that were described as generally related to the primary verbs are replaced by the three-way system of verbal noun and active and passive participles: all agents and adjectives are expressed by the participles, and the passive participles have the additional functions of nouns of time and place and of alternate verbal nouns.

1.5 Non-triliteral forms

1.51 Biliteral forms

Arabic has inherited from Proto-Semitic a number of biliteral roots which retain a marginal place in the noun system, e.g. /yad/ 'hand', as well as traces of even briefer forms which must be padded to function at all and may have a number of variants: /fv̄ (nom. fū, gen. fī, accus. fā)/ ~ /fam/ 'mouth'. Before such roots may be used freely in the derivational system, they must have at least three elements, and many of them have forms in which a /y/ or a /w/ is supplied: /dam/ 'blood', /damiya/ 'bleed'. Because only a small number of genuinely biliteral nouns survive, it is impossible to say how many of the weak verbs of Arabic may originally have been biliteral. One theory maintains the biliteral origin of all Semitic roots, pointing to the existence of series of roots with two consonants (or even one consonant) and semantic content in common.

1.52 Quadriliteral forms: derived nouns and verbs

Both in the noun system and in the verb system, the presence of forms with derivational consonantal affixes and, even more conspicuously, with doubled consonants, means that Arabic has patterns for handling roots with four consonants. For example, the formation of such nouns as /farrūj/ 'chick', root frj, /maktūb/ 'letter', root ktb, and /dukkān/ 'shop', root dkk, all having the general pattern CvCC̄vC and plural CaCāCīC with the actual three consonants of the root variously distributed, allows the language to handle such nouns as /burhān/ 'proof', pl. /barāhīn/, root <u>brhn</u>. Nouns derived from quadriliteral roots are quite common in Arabic, but their variety is limited to forms which can be seen as variants of patterns existing within the triliteral system. The same may be said of the verb system, so that the Form I verb from a quadriliteral root behaves precisely like the Form II verb of a triliteral root: /barhan yubarhin/, etc., except for the verbal noun, which usually follows the nominal pattern CvCC$\bar{a}$C, using all the consonantal slots for members of the root. By the same token, the second quadriliteral form corresponds to the triliteral Form V: /tafalsaf/ 'philosophize, pretend to be a philosopher'. The /n/ affix of the triliteral Form VII is infixed to provide a Form III for the quadriliteral system, whose vowel-consonant pattern ($?$i)CCanCaC corresponds to the triliteral Form X pattern ($?$i)staC_1C_2aC_3: /bran$\check{s}$aq yabran$\check{s}$iq/ 'blossom, flourish', root <u>br$\check{s}$q</u>. A rare fourth form exists, ($?$i)C_1C_2aC_3aC_4C_4, roughly corresponding in pattern to a specialized development of the triliteral Form XI, and in derivation to Form IX.

1.53 <u>The development of quadriliteral forms</u>

An examination of the relationship between roots with three and four consonants reveals the following types of quadriliteral roots:

(a) quadriliteral roots that can be traced to triliteral ones:

    (1) with a repetition of C_1: $C_1C_2C_1C_3$ /qahqar/ 'fall back, retreat', cf. /qahar/ 'defeat';

    (2) with dissimilation of doubled C_2: $C_1C_NC_2C_3$ /faqqaε/, /farqaε/ both 'crack, snap'; C_N may be /r l n y w/;

    (3) with an added fourth consonant: $C_1C_2C_3C_N$ /$\check{s}$amxar/ 'be lofty'; C_N may be /r l s/; cf. /$\check{s}$amax/ 'be lofty';

    (4) with a consonant which was added as part of an identifiable process of derivation treated as if it belonged to the root: /tama<u>dh</u>ab/ 'adhere to a sect', from /ma<u>dh</u>ab/ 'sect, way', a noun of place from /<u>d</u>ahab/ 'go'; here $C_NC_1C_2C_3$;

(b) quadriliteral roots that can be traced to biliteral ones:

$C_1C_2C_1C_2$ /waswas/ 'whisper'; many such verbs have corresponding forms which are triliteral through the doubling of
C_2, or have a third weak consonant: the presence of a few
such verbs which seem to parallel forms with three sound
consonants supports the biliteral theory; many of these
verbs are onomatapoetic: /ġarġar/ 'gargle';

(c) non-reducible quadriliterals $C_1C_2C_3C_4$: many quadriliterals
cannot be reduced to basic sets of two or three consonants;
some must simply be treated as roots with four consonants,
but others may be analyzed in terms of two major processes:

    (1) borrowing (often very ancient): /falsaf/ 'philosophize',
       /ʔamrak/ 'Americanize'; most new quadriliteral verbs
       belong in this class;

    (2) abbreviation: /salεam/ 'say (after any mention of the
       Prophet Muḥammad): /sallā llāhu εalayhi wasallam/ "God
       bless him and grant him salvation"'; /basmal/ 'say:
       /bismi llāh.../ "in the name of God..."'

These processes are all given in terms of verbs, but the development of quadriliterals often takes place in the nominal system
first, especially of types (a) and (c(1)). The complex interaction of the forms may be further demonstrated through such
clusters as: /zall/ 'slip, slide', /zalaq/ 'glide, slide',
/zaḥlaq/ 'roll, slide', /zaḥaf/ 'crawl' (cf. the Hebrew root
ḥlq, which has one form with the meaning 'smooth'), etc. The
interplay of these different roots surely precedes the separate
development of Arabic.

1.6   Outside the root system

Besides the two interlocking systems built up of roots and patterns, the verbal and nominal systems, Arabic has a third system
of particles. Membership in the class of particles is, on the
one hand, a matter of function, since the particles are the words
which do much of the grammatical work of the sentence; on the
other hand, although ties with the root system are occasionally
discernible, particles are words which do not have true roots or

true patterns and are not included in the two inflectional systems. In many cases, especially among the pronouns, they seem
to be composed of monosyllabic elements strung together (often
with alternative long and short forms) to produce words of varying bulk; an analysis from this point of view, especially when
it begins to deal with possibilities of relationships between
such elements and the consonant affixes of the root-based systems,
rapidly becomes speculative and can only be extensive if it is
carried out from a comparative or historical point of view. The
following section is more concerned with giving a range of examples than with an exhaustive coverage.

1.61 Monoliteral and biliteral particles

A small series of particles appear as single unstressed syllables
standing before the word. They are less closely bound to the
word than the inflectional prefixes, and tend to express syntactic
relationships. Among these are the conjunctions /wa-/ 'and'
(implying simultaneity) and /fa-/ 'and' (implying sequence);
/sa-/, which makes an imperfect verb future; /ʔa-/, an interrogative; /la-/, which adds emphasis; /li-/, which introduces a
subjunctive; and the prepositions /bi-/ 'in, by, with', /li- ~
la-/ 'to', /ka-/ 'like', and /wa-/, introducing an oath, which
govern the genitive. A further group of slightly more substan-
tial forms includes: /hal/, an interrogative; /law/ 'if'; the
prepositions /ɛan/ 'from, about'; /fī/ 'in'; /ʔilā ~ ʔilay-/
'to, toward'; etc., going on towards forms which contain recognizable roots.

1.62 Sets of particles

A second way of looking at the particles isolates a number of
families of particles, such as the negations /lā/ for the imperfect, /lam/ (+ verb in the jussive) for the perfect, and /lan/
(+ the subjunctive) for the future. Another such series is
formed by the interrogative (relative) pronouns /mā/ and /mādā/
'what'; /man/ 'who'; /matā/ 'when'. A series of great syntactic
importance is built on the base /n/:

38

Before verbs	Before nouns (accus.) or pronouns
/ʔin/ 'if'	/ʔinna/ 'indeed'
/ʔan/ 'so that'	/ʔanna/ 'that'
/lākin/ 'but'	/lākinna/ 'but'

On this level of complexity, we begin to find a great many particles which are recognizable combinations of two or more particles which exist separately: /kaʔanna/ 'as though' (+ noun); /bilā/ 'without'; /ʔillā/ ← /ʔin/ + /lā/ 'except'; /limādā/ 'why'; etc.

1.63 Pronouns

An examination of the above forms reveals at once the difficulty of dissecting the particles of Arabic without constant historical references. Between the forms which clearly consist of a single element, and those which are clearly compounded of at least two elements (which still have an autonomous existence, strung together at some early date), are a number of sets of particles which seem related in one or more of their elements but cannot readily be analyzed.

The pronouns of Arabic are of special interest, since they present an extensive system of composite forms, syllables, and single consonants strung together, of varying bulk. In many cases, variants have been retained, e.g. /dāka/, /hadāka/, /dālika/ (plus the diminutives /dayyāka/ and /dayyālika/) 'that (masc. sing.)', but only the prevailing modern forms are given in the Tables below.

The Arab grammarians have traditionally treated the pronouns with the nouns rather than with the particles, because of their role in the sentence and because they reflect the obligatory categories of the noun (case, gender, and number). However, they resemble the particles in lying outside the root system, and they indicate gender and number differently, often by vowel contrasts: /huwa/ 'he' vs. /hiya/ 'she'.

1.631 Personal pronouns

The personal pronouns (Table 6) are quite brief, and have some resemblance to the agent affixes of the verb. They have two

STRUCTURE

Table 6
Personal Pronouns

	Isolated form	Suffixed form
3rd person		
Masc. sing.	/huwa/	/-hu/ (~/ -hū/)
Fem. sing.	/hiya/	/-hā/
Masc. pl.	/hum/	/-hum/
Fem. pl.	/hunna/	/-hunna/
Dual	/humā/	/-humā/
2nd person		
Masc. sing.	/ʔanta/	/-ka/
Fem. sing.	/ʔanti/	/-ki/
Masc. pl.	/ʔantum/	/-kum/
Fem. pl.	/ʔantunna/	/-kunna/
Dual	/ʔantumā/	/-kumā/
1st person		
Singular	/ʔanā/	/-(n)iy(a)/
Plural	/naḥnu/	/-nā/

forms, an isolated form which generally refers to the subject of the clause and a suffixed form which replaces either the accusative or the genitive and is suffixed to nouns, verbs, and many particles after their final short vowel. Examples of the use of suffixed forms: /ṭalabtu-hum/ 'I sought them', /nusāɛidu-ka/ 'we will help you'.

The /-(n)-/ of the first person singular is required after verbs and some particles, while the /-iy(a)/ form is used after nouns and obscures the case ending: /bayt-ī/ 'my house' (case unknown) vs. /ṭalabta-nī/ 'you (masc. sing.) sought me'. The final /-(a)/ is required only when the /-iy-/ elides with a /-y/ at the end of the stem; it is optional and rather old-fashioned elsewhere: /ɛalay-/ 'on' + /-iy(a)/ → /ɛalayya/ 'on me'.

The short /u/ of the third person suffixes is replaced by /i/ when it follows /-i/ or /-y/: /bayti-himā/ 'of their (dual) house'.

40

The suffixed pronouns are determining complements, and the nouns to which they are affixed cannot have nunation or the definite article, while duals and sound masculine plurals lose their final -nv: /muslimī-hi/ 'of his Muslims'.

1.632 Demonstrative and relative pronouns

These pronouns, which accompany or replace definite nouns only, are built up from ancient demonstrative elements plus various determining elements and indications of gender and number. The arrangement of the demonstratives /d̲/ (masc.) vs. /t/ (fem.) vs. /l/ (common plural) contrasts with the relative, which retains the /d̲/ vs. /t/ contrast and distinguishes gender in the plural. For the demonstratives, /h/ vs. /k/ expresses near (this) and far (that), and recurs in /hunā/ and /hāhunā/ 'here' vs. /hunāka/, /hunālika/ 'there'. Note also /hākadā/ 'thus'.

The forms given in Table 7 are standard for modern usage, but there are a number of variants—this is one of the areas of Arabic grammar where one is most aware of ancient heterogeneity.

Table 7

Demonstrative and Relative Pronouns

Demonstrative pronouns:

	Singular		Dual		Plural	
	masc.	fem.	masc.	fem.	masc.	fem.
'this'	/hādā/	/hādihi/	/hādāni/	/hātāni/	/hāʔulāʔi/	
'that'	/dālika/	/tilka/	/dānnika/	/tānnika/	/ʔulāʔika/	

Relative pronouns:

'which'	/lladī/	/llatī/	/lladāni/	/llatāni/	/lladīna/	/llāti/

The initial /l/ of the relative pronoun is the definite article, and requires /ʔa-/ after silence (see 1.23). All of the dual forms differentiate between the nominative and other cases by the same vowel alternation as for nouns: /daynnika/ 'those (two)' (gen. or accus.).

In addition to these, Arabic employs the interrogative pronouns as relatives which do not reflect the obligatory categories
of the noun (see 1.62); there are others which do not belong to
this series, especially /ʔayy/ 'whatever, whoever, which', etc.
The suffix /-mā/ often corresponds to English '-ever': /ʔaynamā/
'wherever'.

1.7 Syntax

Any complete description of Arabic syntax would go far beyond
the scope of this structural sketch; for brevity, we must be concerned with interesting or pivotal features of Arabic syntax,
rather than with the attempt to present it as a coherent system.
We shall be concerned here with (a) the relationship between the
three categories (nouns, verbs, and particles) which have been
necessary for a formal description of Arabic, and the more elaborate system of 'parts of speech' which might be expected on the
basis of a conventional training in English grammar; (b) the
major sentence, clause, and phrase types; and (c) the functions
of the case and modal endings.

1.71 Parts of speech

Nouns and verbs are distinguished in Arabic (a) derivationally,
because different sets of patterns may be ascribed to each class;
(b) inflectionally, because different kinds of affixes are joined
to each (verbs indicate person, nouns indicate definiteness and
case, and there is only a partial similarity between the way the
two systems indicate gender and number); and (c) functionally,
in terms of the syntactic roles they can play in the sentence.

The role played by the verb has relatively few surprises for
the speaker of English: Arabic employs special (usually non-
verbal) constructions in place of some English uses of the verb
'to have' and the present of the verb 'to be', and tends to out-
do English in using verbs to describe states: Arabic prefers 'he
grieves' or 'he rages' to 'he is unhappy', 'he is angry'.

The noun, on the other hand, fills a number of functions which
are associated with a greater specialization in English. Although

there is some separation in terms of derivational patterns, the
remarks on nominal inflection (see 1.3) apply to words which
fill roles corresponding to the following English categories:

(a) Substantives: /bayt/ 'house', /hind/ 'Hind (a woman's name)',
/lištirākīyah/ '(the) socialism'.

(b) Adjectives, including participles and comparatives-superla-
tives: /karīm/ 'noble, generous', /kātib/ 'writing', /ʔakbar/
'bigger, biggest'. These forms, when used syntactically to
express attributes, follow the noun and agree with it in
gender, number and determination, but they may also stand
alone: /karīm/ 'a noble or generous man, Karīm (a man's
name)', /kātib/ 'scribe, secretary', /kātibah/ 'secretary
(fem.)', /ʔakbar/ 'Akbar (a man's name)', /lʔakbar/ 'the
greatest (one)'. Nor is it useful to speak of an adjectival
inflection 'big, bigger, biggest', since comparative-superla-
tive forms often exist in direct relationship with the verb
without reference to an adjectival base form. There is some
morphological justification for setting up a class of adjectives on the basis of the partial specialization of derivational forms, the ease with which feminine endings may be
applied, and the specialization of plurals: participles and
relative adjectives generally take sound plurals, and even
where they have broken plurals, these are more predictable
than broken plurals of nouns. When the use of first form
participles as substantives crystallizes, they acquire
specialized broken plurals: /rrijālu l-kātibūn/ 'the writing
men' vs. /lkuttāb/ 'the scribes'.

(c) Adverbs: In Arabic there is no real class of adverbs corresponding to the English one. Arabic has a number of adverbial
particles, e.g. /faqaṭ/ 'only, no more', which follows the
verb, but most of the load carried in English by adverbs is
carried in Arabic by nouns in the accusative (see 1.72):
/lyawm/ 'the day', /lyawma/ 'today'; /sarīɛ/ 'swift',
/sarīɛan/ 'swiftly'; /dāʔim/ 'continuing' (active participle
of /dām/ 'continue'), /dāʔiman/ 'always'.

(d) Prepositions: In addition to the monoliteral and biliteral prepositions discussed above (see 1.6), most of the 'prepositions' of Arabic are actually nouns with identifiable roots, which are in the accusative because they are filling an adverbial function and are determined by a following genitive: /qabla ḥarbin/ 'before a war', /fawqa lʔarḍi/ 'above the ground'. The roots appear in other forms: /qabil/ 'receive', /fāq/ 'surpass'; and they may take the diminutive: /fuwayqa lʔarḍi/ 'just above the ground'; or stand alone as adverbs: /qablan/ 'previously'. However, there is some justification for separating a group of these 'prepositions' from the general class of nouns, since they do also appear adverbially with the fossil Semitic adverbial ending /-u/: /qablu/ and even /min qablu/ 'previously'; never take the definite article; and may be followed by /ʔan/ to introduce a clause.

1.72 Major clause types

Although Arabic is an inflected language, it does have a relatively rigid word order which allows for stylistic deviations. The two major clause types of Arabic are differentiated by the presence or absence of a verb.

Verbal clauses have the basic order:

+ verb ± subject ± object ± adverbial(s)

(a) The form of the verb itself indicates the person of the subject: /qataltu/ 'I killed'; and may include a pronominal object: /qataltu-hu/ 'I killed him'; so that Arabic verbs, unlike English verbs, readily form single-word sentences. No modification need be made in this pattern for passive verbs, except that they do not have direct objects (unless the active form was doubly or triply transitive), since passive verbs in Arabic, unlike those of English, cannot have a stated agent. The verb may be preceded by a conjunction, and the verb position may be filled by a verb phrase consisting of a verb plus one or more particles which normally precede it; the two sets of verb forms (perfect vs.

imperfect) provided by the morphology are supplemented by more detailed syntactic indications of present vs. future, especially in negative sentences and within subordinate clauses:

	AFFIRMATIVE	NEGATIVE	
PAST	/qad/ + perf.	/mā/ + perf.	
		/lam/ + juss.	
PRESENT		/mā/ + imperf.	/lā/ + imperf.
FUTURE	/sa-/ + imperf.	/sawfa lā/ + imperf.	
	/sawfa/ + imperf.	/lan/ + subj.	

(b) The subject, if it is present, may be a noun or noun phrase, or a personal or demonstrative pronoun, or even a relative pronoun if a subordinate clause is to follow: /māta lwaladu lkabīru/ 'the big boy died', /māta lladīna qataltu-hum/ 'the ones whom I killed (them) died'. Independent personal pronominal subjects of verbs are rare and introduced only for emphasis. The subject must be in the nominative, and must, if it is a phrase, be endocentric—that is, it must include at least one word, usually in the initial position, which could stand alone as subject. If a stated subject follows the verb, the verb agrees with it only in gender, whereas all subsequent verbs, pronouns, or adjectives referring to it must agree in gender and number; if, however, no subject is stated, the sentence may begin with a plural verb, and all subsequent agreement will be with the implied subject: /qatala rrijālu/ 'the men killed' vs. /qatalū/ 'they killed'. (In this context it is worth repeating that normally the plurals of all words not referring to rational beings are grammatically feminine singular.)

(c) The remaining constituents of the clause, if they are nouns or endocentric noun phrases, must be in the accusative; however, there may be a clause or a particle standing alone or introducing a clause or a noun phrase. Direct objects precede adverbials: /kataba lwaladu lmaktūba lyawma/ 'the boy wrote the letter today' has verb-subject-object-adverbial; /dāma lwaladu karīman/ 'the boy remained noble', /dāma lwaladu bi-lbayti/ 'the boy remained in the house', and /dāma lwaladu yaktubu/ 'the boy continued to write', provide examples of an accusative complement, a phrase introduced by a particle, and a clause consisting of a single imperfect verb.

Arabic also has a type of clause without any verb. These clauses have the order:

+ subject + complement ± adverbial(s)

The positions of complement and adverbial may be filled by the same forms as those listed under (c) above, except that the complement, if it is an endocentric noun phrase, must be nominative. The subject, like the subject of a verbal clause, must be endocentric; however, nominal clauses are much more likely to have pronominal subjects, and their subjects may be accusative if they are introduced by certain particles.

Nominal clauses are frequently translated into English with the present tense of the verb 'to be': /lwaladu fī-lbayti lyawma/ 'the boy is in the house today', /baytu-hu kabīrun/ 'his house is big'.

In the simplest case, where the complement is an indefinite noun (including most adjectives in this position) or is not nominal and the subject is definite, there is no difficulty in dividing the sentence. However, where both are definite: */rrajulu lmaliku/ 'the man is the king'; or indefinite: */mulūkun kirāmun/ 'kings are generous', a third person pronoun may be interposed as a copula: /rrajulu huwa lmaliku/ 'the man, he is the king'; or a particle may be set before the subject which makes it accusative: /ʔinna rrajula lmaliku/ 'indeed, the man is the king'. Such particles are very frequent, and are

46

often necessary for some other aspect of the meaning. Where the
subject is indefinite and the complement is prepositional, many
such clauses translate English 'there is' and are then reversed:
/bi-lbayti waladun/ 'there is a boy in the house', or /ɛindī
maktūbun/ 'I have a letter' (lit., 'there is a letter with me').

Subordinate clauses may be introduced at a number of different
points, and many would be accounted for by a fuller discussion of
the particles, which would have to deal with the problem of interpreting the tense of the verb in the subordinate clause in
relation to that of the main clause. Two types are worth special
notice:

(a) The hāl ('circumstantial') clause: The position of circumstantial complement may be filled by a clause usually introduced by /wa-/ 'and', which here acts as a subordinating
particle (sometimes accompanied by other markers, especially
/qad/ for the perfect), translated 'while, when, although,
but,' etc., which requires that the tense of the verb it
governs be interpreted in relation to the main clause:
/kataba maktūban wahuwa malikun/ 'he wrote a letter while
(or although) he was king'; /sayastaqbilunī waqad qaraʔa
maktūbī/ 'he will receive me now that he has read my letter'.
(b) The relative clause: this must always contain a pronominal
reference to the noun it modifies in the main clause, but
there is no relative pronoun if the noun modified is indefinite: /kataba maktūbayni qabiltu-humā/ 'he wrote two
letters which I received'; /kataba rajulun māta lyawma
maktūban/ 'a man who died today wrote a letter' (lit., 'he
wrote - a man - he died today - a letter'). If the relative clause refers to a definite noun, that noun is followed
by a relative pronoun agreeing with it in number and gender:
/kataba rrajulu lladī māta lyawma maktūban/ 'the man who
died today wrote a letter'. The relative is a member of the
main clause, from which it takes its case, and may stand
alone: /kataba lladī māta.../ 'the one who died wrote...'

1.73 Major types of noun phrases

In endocentric noun phrases, the member of the phrase that could
stand alone usually stands first and shows the case that fits
its role in the sentence. It may be modified by another noun
acting as an adjective which agrees with it grammatically in
number, gender, and definiteness: /lbaytu lkabīru/ 'the big
house', /kātibatun karīmatun/ 'a noble secretary (fem.)', /bi-
bayti-hi lkabīri/ 'in his large house'. It may be followed by
a genitive determining complement in the idāfa ('construct'):
the first member of a construct phrase cannot have nunation or
the definite article and is generally determined by the following noun, so that any subsequent adjective modifying it directly
must be definite: /baytu lkātibati lkabīru/ 'the large house of
the secretary (fem.)'. Occasionally, if the second member is
indefinite, the first may be treated as indefinite: /maktūbu
rajulin/ may be 'the letter of a man' or 'a letter of a man'.
Construct phrases are treated like words—they have only a
single marker of determination (on the last member) and a single
marker of their role in the sentence (on the first); thus, they
may be in construct to still another noun, and adjectives modifying any member of the construct phrase must follow. Constructs
express more than possession, as the following examples show:
/karīmu nnafsi/ 'noble of soul', /ʔakbaru madīnatin/ 'greatest
of cities', /qabla lḥarbi/ 'before the war'. A construct modifying a definite noun may have an initial definite article:
/lmaliku lkarīmu nnafsi/ 'the king noble of soul'.

1.74 The role of the case and modal endings

On the basis of the previous discussion, it is clear that the
loss of final short vowels in all dialects of Arabic, and the
fact that these are not indicated in the writing and are only
pronounced in context forms (see 1.24), must be considered in
relation to their relatively minor importance in Classical
Arabic. It has hardly been necessary to discuss the use of the
modes, since these are mainly marked by specific particles and
the vast majority of unmarked verbs are indicative. Among the

nouns, the fact that determination is indicated only on the second member of the construct and that the word order in the phrase is not variable is generally sufficient to mark this type of phrase, while all other genitives are associated with prepositions. So long as the order described above is maintained, there is little difficulty in distinguishing functions marked by the nominative and genitive case. Writers of Classical Arabic differ in the extent to which they deviate from this order and exploit stylistically the flexibility of word order which is present in theory. Many stylistic devices which make it possible to stress some element besides the verb may be analyzed in terms of the word order described here, particularly the use of a nominal sentence with a clause as its complement: /ʔinna lmalikata māta ṣadīquhā/ 'indeed, the queen [is a person who] her friend died' (instead of /māta ṣadīqu l-malikati/ 'the queen's friend died').

NOTES

1. Charles A. Ferguson, 'The Emphatic l in Arabic', Language 32.446-52 (1956).

2. Joseph H. Greenberg, 'The Patterning of Root Morphemes in Semitic', Word 6.162-81 (1950).

3. Henri Fleisch, S.J., L'Arabe classique: Esquisse d'une structure linguistique (Beirut, 1956), from which Table 2 is adapted.

2. THE HISTORY OF CLASSICAL ARABIC

2.1 The Semitic family of languages

Arabic is a member of a family of languages which have been
spoken for millennia in areas where Arabic is now in use or in
immediately adjacent areas. These languages are called Semitic
languages and their interrelationship is evident from similar-
ities of structure which make it possible to reconstruct a par-
ent language, Proto-Semitic, from which they are all descended.
Semitic languages still in use are, besides Arabic: Ethiopic,
especially as Amharic, the modern language of Ethiopia; the
South Arabic languages, a group of languages including Mehrī
and Soqotrī, spoken by a small population in the south of
Arabia; Hebrew, the language of the state of Israel, which had
fallen from use as a spoken language for over two thousand years
until its revival by the Zionists; Aramaic, spoken in a cluster
of villages in the Anti-Lebanon north of Damascus, and its near
relation, Syriac, spoken by groups in Iran and Iraq. Arabic
(sometimes called Northern Arabic for greater clarity) is by
far the most important Semitic language, with over eighty million speakers.

Arabic, Ethiopic, and the South Arabic languages are especially closely related, forming a cluster or sub-grouping known
as South (or Southwest) Semitic, and our knowledge of them is
comparatively recent. In contrast, Akkadian, the long-dead language of the Assyrian and early Babylonian Empires, is known
from approximately 2500 B.C.; with the various forms and regional
dialects it developed before it died out completely about A.D.
100, Akkadian is considered to be a separate, Eastern branch of
Semitic, set apart from the Western branches by a highly deviant
verbal inflection, a simplified phonology, and the use of š in
a number of morphological positions where other Semitic languages
have ḥ ~ ?.

The remaining Semitic languages have usually been classed as the Western or Northwestern group: the Canaanite dialects, including Hebrew, the languages of a number of other peoples mentioned in the Old Testament, and Phoenician, which was an important commercial language, later the language of Carthage, form one branch; and Aramaic, the language spoken in Palestine at the time of Christ and the later administrative language of Babylon (the Eastern branch of Aramaic is called Syriac) forms the other.

These are quite rough groupings and there is considerable dispute about the precise relationships between these languages and groups of languages. The first inscriptions in West Semitic only go back to 1400 B.C., so it is hard to specify its relationship to Akkadian, although reconstructions of older fragments of a language called Amorite provide some hints of a link. Ugaritic, written in cuneiform on clay tablets which were discovered at Ras Shamra in 1929, has stimulated new discussions of the relationships within West Semitic. There is, however, no doubt of the general pattern of relationships, as all of these languages are characterized by a series of consonants corresponding to the emphatic and emphatic-like consonants of Arabic and a morphology based on triliteral consonant roots interlocking with derivational patterns. Semitic itself is a member of the Hamito-Semitic (Afro-Asiatic) superfamily, which includes Egyptian (from Ancient Egyptian to Coptic), Libico-Berber, and the Cushitic languages. Here the precise relationships are even more difficult to determine.

Among the Semitic languages, Arabic is conspicuous as showing the features that characterize Semitic in a very fully realized form—that is to say, it has a rich inventory of consonants and a highly elaborated system of derivation from the triliteral root. Semiticists differ on whether this was true of Proto-Semitic and has been blurred in the other Semitic languages, or whether the system was originally much more rudimentary and has in Arabic simply been pushed, by analogy, towards its logical conclusion. This seems to be the case, for example, of the derived verbs. Akkadian has four forms (primary, geminate, causative with š equivalent to Arabic /ʔa-/ in Form IV, and passive with n); each of these may have infixed t, tan, or tata (although the last, especially, is very rare). By including fossilized forms, it can be shown that Ethiopic has a very symmetrical system in which each one of the three forms produced without affixes (qatala, qattala, and qātala) appears alone and with each possible affix (e.g. qatala yields qatala, aqtala, astaqtala, and taqatla; and so on for the three others). Since Arabic also has a number of rare forms that were omitted in the preceding structural sketch, any attempt to postulate a system for Proto-Semitic which exploits all the derivational devices surviving in the attested languages results in almost twenty types. This is probably a case where, starting from a system which included a tendency toward this type of derivation, the different languages have produced different analogous elaborations. Classical Arabic is the only language with a full set of passives made by vowel alternation and has a very complex system, while the Northwest Semitic languages have quite simple ones. The case seems to be much the same with the pronouns, since the same components appear in all of them, with the same gender distinctions (in the demonstratives, for example, ḏ (~[z]) for the singular, t for the feminine and l for the plural), but the forms are variously augmented, and the partial use of vowels to distinguish gender varies greatly. In Ethiopic, the use of -k in second person pronominal suffixes has been extended to the agent suffixes of verbs, e.g. qatalka, second person masculine singular perfect.

Arabic phonology is very close to the reconstructed phonology of Proto-Semitic. Proto-Semitic *p > Arabic /f/ and Proto-Semitic *g > Arabic /j/, which patterns as the voiced consonant corresponding to /š/ instead of /k/, causing some realignment in the system. The complicated system of Proto-Semitic sibilants is shuffled, and Arabic /s/ represents the merger of two different Proto-Semitic phonemes. In contrast to this, all the other

Semitic languages except Ugaritic have lost a number of phonemes, especially the interdentals and the consonants formed toward the back of the mouth (e.g. in Akkadian, Proto-Semitic *ʔ, *ġ, *ḥ, *ɛ, and *h as well as *y and *w are all realized as ʔ). The Arabic vowel system, with three vowel positions and phonemic length, seems to preserve the original system, but colloquial dialects share the trend of other Semitic languages to develop phonemic stress and increase the number of vowels.

In general, features of Arabic grammar which are notably conservative have often been lost in the colloquials, which have in many cases developed in directions attested in earlier forms of other Semitic languages. One area in which a degree of complexity retained in Arabic has often been lost elsewhere is inflection for number; the dual especially has tended to be limited to a few frozen forms, just as dual verbal and pronominal forms have tended to disappear in the colloquial. Furthermore, although modern Classical Arabic stands somewhere between an aspect system and a tense system, this evolution has been completed in a number of Semitic languages and in some colloquial forms of Arabic, often with the generalization of the active participle as a present tense. In the same way, the loss of final short vowels and nunation (mimation, with m instead of n, in other Semitic languages), which characterizes the shift from Classical to Colloquial Arabic, occurred much earlier in other offshoots of Semitic.

2.2   The Arabic writing system

Unlike some of the related languages (Egyptian, attested by hieroglyphs from 3000 B.C., and Akkadian, first attested in 2400 B.C.), the earliest clearly Arabic inscriptions are dated as A.D. 512 and 568, and there is no abundance of written records until well into the Islamic period. The peoples of Arabia had first contacted writing as it was used in the Mediterranean empires, primarily for Aramaic. At an early period, the speakers of South Arabic in the Sabaean kingdom of Yemen adopted one of

the early Canaanite alphabets for their own use, with twenty-
nine letters without ligatures. Inscriptions in this orthography have been found in various parts of Arabia (Liḥyānic,
Thamūdic, and Ṣafāitic), and it now serves, after a number of
radical changes, as the writing system of Ethiopia. Speakers of
Arabic began to use the Aramaic alphabet (with forms very like
those of modern Hebrew) as early as the beginning of the Christian era, but they wrote in Aramaic. This usage developed in two
Arab kingdoms which had brief periods of power, the Nabatean
kingdom at Petra, which was conquered by Rome in 106, and Palmyra,
conquered in 273, but the so-called Sinaitic inscriptions were
being made by Nabateans until as late as A.D. 300. Over the
years, more and more Arabic forms from the spoken language fil-
tered into writing, and a certain number of ligatures begin to
appear between the slowly simplified forms of the letters. The
modern Arabic script is descended from this Nabatean script,
which was subjected to a number of modifications to suit the
phonology of Arabic.

The Nabatean alphabet fell short of meeting the needs of
Arabic in a number of ways. First of all, Arabic has a number
of consonants which do not occur in Aramaic: $/t/$, $/d/$, $/ḥ/$, $/ġ/$,
$/ẓ/$, and $/ḍ/$. Second, the simplification of the letter forms
and the introduction of ligatures to form a cursive script had
resulted in the loss of a number of distinctions which had existed previously; for instance, a small tooth or wiggle in the
line of script had to represent the consonants $/b/$, $/t/$, $/n/$,
and $/y/$, as well as the Arabic phoneme $/t/$ (because of its similarity to $/t/$). For some positions in the word, the Arabic
alphabet had only fifteen letter shapes to represent twenty-eight
consonant phonemes. This made reading extremely difficult, and
various solutions were experimented with even before the rise of
Islam in the seventh century A.D. The oldest written records in
Islam—coins from the middle of the seventh century, inscriptions
on tombs and milestones soon after, and papyruses by the end of
that century—show that dots were already beginning to be placed

above or below the letters, in groups of one, two, or three, to
distinguish identically written consonants. The system was not
completely worked out for another hundred years: dots were used
sporadically and inconsistently and some of the conventions used
at the time (for /f/ and /q/) were later changed. From about the
middle of the eighth century on, however, the use of the dots as
necessary and regular parts of the letters was stabilized and the
undotted script was only used for decorative inscriptions.

Like other Semitic alphabets, however, the adapted Nabatean
used by the Arabs is purely consonantal. This is appropriate to
the structure of the Semitic languages, where most of the meaning
is lodged in the consonantal skeleton of the word, particularly
in the root, and the vowels can usually be deduced; in fact,
transcriptions of Arabic, such as that used in the present study,
tend to blur the basic structure of grammatical forms. When long
vowels were analyzed as short vowel plus semivowel, as they eventually were in the more evolved forms of most Semitic alphabets,
the semivowel was written, with the result that parts of the consonantal structure which had tended to be lost in the earliest
orthography were restored and a number of important grammatical
distinctions made possible. In the modern Arabic alphabet, the
letters wāw and yā? (/w/ and /y/) are used to indicate /ū/ and
/ī/, and /aw/ and /ay/ as well, and the alif (or occasionally
yā? in final position) to indicate /ā/. Alif is also used to
indicate prosthetic syllables, and some word divisions. Since
alif had originally represented a phoneme (the glottal stop /ʔ/),
a new sign had to be invented for this, and after some experimentation the grammarians settled on a sign called hamza, a small
version of the initial form of the letter ɛayn (/ɛ/). This sign
was integrated into the sequence of letters by being set on one
of them as a support. Alif is the most frequent support, but
later wāw and yā? were pressed into service if the glottal stop
was followed or preceded by /u/ or /i/. Choosing a support for
hamza is complicated, but once chosen it gives some information
about the short vowel environment. At about the same time, a

miniature /š/ called <u>shadda</u> was adopted to stand over doubled consonants. Although the <u>hamza</u> and <u>shadda</u> are not consistently indicated, they are considered part of the script and are written in the same ink as the basic letter forms.

Arabic is written from right to left in a graceful, highly cursive script. All the letters may be attached to a preceding letter but there are six which are never joined to a following letter. Many of the letters have special forms after a space, they are at their simplest when connected left and right, and most of the letters are provided with loops at the end of the word. The positional variation in letter shapes indicates word separation, and there is nothing equivalent to our system of capitalization. These elements, with the additional strokes which three letters require for their basic shape, make up the cursive line of Arabic.

However appropriate the consonantal system was, a study of the preceding grammatical sketch will show that there are many in-stances of ambiguities which can only be resolved by specifying the short vowels. Even before the invention of <u>hamza</u> and <u>shadda</u>, the Arabs experimented with the use of dots for short vowels— placed above a consonant followed by /a/, in the letter for /u/, and below it for /i/. These were distinguished from the con-sonantal dots by the use of colored inks, usually red, while the cursive line was written in black. The use of red ink for vowel marking, along with the association of the position with par-ticular vowels, continued after the adoption of new vowel signs (attributed to the grammarian al-Khalīl) which were small, sim-plified versions of the letters <u>alif</u>, <u>wāw</u>, and <u>yāʔ</u>. These are doubled to indicate nunation. This system was in use by the middle of the eighth century for the Qur'ān, where accuracy was vital. Its use is still limited to the Qur'ān, poetry, child-ren's books, and occasional helpful hints at points where con-fusion is very likely. The vowels are not indicated in the normal printing of books and newspapers or in medieval prose manuscripts.

Arabs are very conscious of the beauties of calligraphy and have developed a number of decorative scripts (especially Kūfī and Thuluth); the frequent use of writing for decoration is partly linked to the prohibition on pictorial representation. Arabs write between, rather than on the lines, and achieve a straight left margin and other aesthetic balance by the extreme lengthening of some letter forms. Commentaries, or even totally separate books, are often written in the margins. The commonest of the scripts which were developed for use on papyrus is called naskhī and is now used for most Arabic printing; this hand is frequently taught to Westerners, although most Arabs east of Tripolitania use the so-called ruqεa script for handwriting, a simplified script developed for chancellory use. Various scripts are used for printing and handwriting in North Africa; /f/ and /q/ are dotted somewhat differently, and Sudanese writing is considered thick and clumsy, while Algerian is unusually angular.

The Arab conquests and the spread of Islam caused the spread of Arabic and of the Arabic alphabet. Almost all Muslim peoples have used the alphabet at some time or other; in addition to Arabic, it has been used for Persian (and other Iranian languages), Osmanli, the Turkish of Turkey (and other Turkic languages, including Uighur and Kazakh), Urdu, and Malay. In Africa it has been used for Berber (except by the Tuaregs), Swahili, Hausa, dialects in the area of Lake Chad, and occasional others. Osmanli, Malay, and all Turkic in use in Communist China have adapted Latin alphabets, while the Arabic alphabet has been replaced in the Soviet Union, after experiments with various Latin alphabets, by modified Cyrillic. Iran and Pakistan are the two most important non-Arabic-speaking countries using the Arabic script today, and both of these use a script called nestaεlīq (often called taεlīq in the West). Nestaεlīq is a jagged script, heavily influenced by the old Pahlevi (an early form of Persian) orthography; the word slopes down towards the end (the left), with long-drawn-out final loops. Because it is more difficult to print, it is being replaced by naskhī in Pakistani use, beginning with the newspapers.

The system of dots was extended to distinguish consonants which occur in these other languages ([p], [č], [g], etc.) and these are now occasionally used in Arabic for unassimilated loanwords. Arabic consonant letters which did not reflect pho-nemic differences in the borrowing languages were generally re-tained in words borrowed from Arabic. The consonantal alphabet of Arabic is not appropriate to the Turkic and Indo-European languages that have used it; it tends to make reading difficult and to favor the readily recognizable Arabic loanwords. Turkish, which has a complicated system of vowels and vowel harmony, used the symbols for the emphatic consonants to indicate the presence of back vowels, but this was a makeshift and imperfect technique.

2.3 Arabic literature

2.31 Pre-Islamic literature and the Qur'ān

The history of Arabic literature begins in the sixth century with the highly institutionalized uses of poetry in the tribal society of Arabia. Since then, Arabic has been first the language of a vast Islamic empire, then one of many Islamic languages, retain-ing its special privileges only in areas directly related to religion, and finally the language of a number of nation states entering the modern world and responding to its aesthetics as well as to its technology and political ideology. The need to keep Classical Arabic, as the vehicle of the religious tradition, as 'pure' as possible was in constant tension with the struggle to adapt this language, which was probably never in general use, to new didactic and expressive aims. Both of these pressures have tended to reinforce a stress on form rather than content which began in the pre-Islamic period.

In the century before Islam, poetic forms were already highly developed, and the role of the poet was an important one. His poetry was public and on his eloquence depended the honor of the tribe and the mockery of their enemies. In the most elaborate form of composition, the qaṣīda ('ode'), the poet would follow a stylized sequence of themes, establishing his poetic authority by his skill in describing the traces left at an abandoned encampment and his nostalgia for some romance that took place there, followed by a journey or description of his horse or camel, reflecting his own valor. After this preparation, he would conclude the poem with a political or a personal statement, often a panegyric. A number of metrical forms, based on the alternation of long and short syllables, were available to him, and the same rhyme had to be maintained on all the fifty to a hundred lines of the poem. A similar form, but without the rigid sequence of themes, was used for elegies, and a nonmetrical rhymed prose, sajε, seems to have been used by soothsayers and for proverbs.

These forms seem to represent the main uses of the poetic language in formal, intertribal communication, and they possessed the authority, always very high for the Arabs, of eloquence. When Muḥammad began the revelation of the Qur'ān in A.D. 610, a process which continued until his death in 632, he was compared to both poets and soothsayers, who were believed to be possessed by demons, and had to defend the special divinely inspired nature of his words even as he was slowly finding new resources of style for the expression of novel ideas. Because he was accused of being a poet, he spoke very harshly of poetry in general. The early sūras (chapters) are very lyrical, quite short, and contain elements of both poetry and sajε, but the later ones, composed when Muḥammad was governing and legislating for the city of Medina, to which he had fled in 622 (A.H. 1, the first year of the Muslim era), are the earliest evidence we have of Arabic prose, and were probably cast in a style developed by Muḥammad himself, although the stylistic development has been obscured by the arbitrary arrangement of sūras in the canonical form of the Qur'ān.

Subsequently, a large proportion of Arabic literary effort was to be devoted to the interpretation of the Qur'ān, making use of pre-Islamic poetry as linguistic evidence, but there were great differences in composition and preservation between the two forms.

The odes seem to have been composed by professional poets who, although capable of improvising, would often labor long over a poem and generally composed the passages dealing with single themes as unified wholes, memorizing them themselves or reciting them to professional reciters, who were often 'apprentice poets', who would commit them to memory section by section for public recitation. This oral tradition maintained considerable linguistic homogeneity within a standard 'poetic language' and preserved lengthy poems for two centuries and more. Muḥammad, on the other hand, had had no such apprenticeship, so that his use of the poetic language is tinged by the local usage of the Quraysh tribe of Mecca. Supposedly, he recited sections of the Book just as he received them from the Archangel Gabriel, with little or no polishing. In this case, the memorization was done by a number of people or fragmentary passages were recorded on whatever writing materials were available, which were then transmitted back and forth between the Companions of the Prophet, each trying to expand the portion of the text he knew by heart and supplementing it by a developing tradition of exchanging accounts of the Prophet's words or doings (hadīth). The practice of memorizing the Qur'ān is still a common one, but in the warfare that accompanied the spread of Islam too many of the Companions were being killed, and the first Caliph (successor to the Prophet), Abū Bakr, had a complete manuscript prepared in 633, which was revised under the Caliph ɛUthmān in 651 and put into its final form. Since the early Arabic script did not indicate vowels, oral tradition was still necessary to determine readings of the Qur'ān, often making a great difference of meaning. This left a loophole for dispute and uncertainty which was not closed until the reign of ɛAbd al-Malik (685-705) when the diacritical marks were introduced, reflecting a reading of the Qur'ān which shows a slight normalization of Qurayshite usage.

2.32 Umayyad literature

During the first four 'orthodox' caliphates and under the Umayyad dynasty of caliphs who ruled the empire from Damascus from 661 to

750, literary production was small. Poetry survived Muḥammad's disapproval and continued in the pre-Islamic tradition except for a shift in values and a tendency to break down the ode into more occasional pieces (love songs, wine songs). In Syria, three rival poets, al-Akhṭal, al-Farazdaq, and Jarīr, abused each other in verse, skillfully and often obscenely. In Mecca, which had become a very gay city under the impact of the pilgrimages and the revenue they brought, poetry, especially love poetry, was set to music, while in Medina, a much soberer city, in which the Muslim sciences were beginning to develop, a parallel tradition of love poetry developed; instead of the gay poems of coquetry and seduction written by ɛUmar b. Abī Rabīɛa at Mecca, Medina produced near epics of disappointed love. Meanwhile, an oral tradition, especially in the garrison cities of Iraq, dealt with accumulated teachings about the life of the Prophet and the best interpretation of the Book. A great part of the literary production of the ɛAbbāsid dynasty which followed consisted of the writing down of materials which had crystallized in spoken form in the previous era and the collection of pre-Islamic poetry which was still memorized and recited in town and desert.

2.33 ɛAbbāsid literature

2.331 The Islamic sciences

The ɛAbbāsid dynasty was established in 750. The ɛAbbāsids based their power on Islam, rather than identifying with the Arabs, and moved their capital to Baghdad, where they were enriched by the creativity of Persian converts to Islam. The dynasty flourished for about a hundred years (the famous reign of Hārūn al-Rashīd (786-809) falls in this period), and then came to lean more and more on Praetorian guards of slave-soldiers. Local governments became increasingly autonomous, and there was a long period of decline. The Classical Age of Arabic literature, which began under the ɛAbbāsids and continued under other local dynasties, ends with the sack of Baghdad by the Mongols in 1258. During the ɛAbbāsid period, literature was tremendously stimulated by the generous patronage of a court which was fully alive to its possibilities for entertainment and its utility in the search for clear and final formulations on points of religious controversy and in the induction of new converts into Islamic and Arabic civilization. Translations from Persian and from Greek, via Syriac, provided an additional stimulus, and the establishment of a paper factory in Baghdad in 795 made it possible to write and own many books and to transfer the oral tradition to written form.

The need for clarification of religious questions led to the development of the Muslim sciences of Qur'ānic exegesis, law, and tradition (hadīth). Qur'ānic exegesis depended on a knowledge of Arabic grammar, which was being investigated at Baṣra and Kūfa, the garrison cities of Iraq. In these new cities, scholars who were often of Persian origin gathered linguistic data by collecting the ancient poetry and by questioning Bedouins, who were thought to speak a purer form of Arabic. The main collections of poetry were written down between 750 and 900, and a number of anthologies were put together. One of the most famous of these, al-Muεallaqāt, included one poem each by seven of the foremost pre-Islamic poets: Imru'u 1-Qays (famous for a long section describing amorous intrigues, and for the description of a storm with which it closes), Ṭarafa (with at least forty lines of description of his camel), Zuhayr (preaching against war), Labīd, εAntara, εAmr b. Kulthūm, and Hārith b. Ḥilliza. Other anthologies included shorter poems as well as complete odes, and two of the most famous, which were arranged by topics, bear the same title, Ḥamāsa [Fortitude], for their first and longest section. These were compiled by Abū Tammām (d. 850), himself a poet, and al-Buḥturī (d. 897). While some philologists became so fascinated by the study of the ancient poetry that this became a separate branch of learning, others were formulating the rules of Arabic grammar, culminating in the great work of Sibawayh, called simply al-Kitāb [The Book].

The study of history also developed to meet religious needs. The mass of lore about the life and sayings of the Prophet, each anecdote being supported by a chain of authority by which it had ostensibly been passed on from the Companions of the Prophet, was used as a source of doctrine. When heterodox tendencies developed in Islam, traditions supporting all sorts of contradictory dogmas were attributed to Muḥammad and the chains of authority (isnād) forged, so that a science of hadīth developed to identify them. Six collections of traditions were eventually accepted as genuine (ṣaḥīḥ), of which the first two by al-Bukhārī (d. 870) and Muslim (d. 874) are the most important. Traditions relating to Muḥammad's life had been woven into a continuous narrative (the Sīra) by Ibn Isḥāq in the eighth century (written down in the ninth), stories of the conquest (maghāzī) were collected at the same time, and the type of reference work (ṭabaqāt 'categories') which was to become so common in Islam, with entries on long lists of scholars, poets, etc., was invented by Ibn Saεd (d. 845) when he wrote Kitābu l-ṭabaqāti l-kabīr classifying all the Companions of the Prophet with their lives and genealogies and criteria for determining the authenticity of hadīth. By the time of al-Ṭabarī (d. 922) history was established as a separate science, and it was possible for this scholar to write a commentary on the Qur'ān, which served as the basis for most later exegesis, and a universal history to illuminate the revelation of God's purpose through world events. The History of Prophets and Kings of al-Ṭabarī is written much like a collection of traditions: each fact or point of view is supported by a chain of authority, and several versions of the same event are set side by side, without being integrated in a continuous narrative, beginning with the creation of the world and concentrating on the history of the Islamic empire. History continued to be a major concern of Arabic literature, but although later works are mines of information about particular provinces or dynasties, no historian as interesting as al-Ṭabarī appeared until the fourteenth century.

2.332 Belles lettres

Another literary genre, known as adab ('belles lettres'),

developed for those audiences, especially those around the court, that were concerned with combining edification with amusement and with obtaining enough information on any subject to appear educated. Such writings were especially useful to the class of secretaries and bureaucrats, primarily of non-Arab origin, who needed induction into Islamic civilization and models on which to base their style. Adab stemmed from a concern with philology, with increasing elaboration of the background material necessary for literacy, and finally came to range from pure entertainment to popularizations of difficult subjects, covering a spectrum about as wide as that which appears in the pages of today's New Yorker magazine, and often acted as the medium in which the tension between Arabism and the ethnic consciousness (shuεūbīya) of the non-Arab converts was expressed.

On the purely entertainment side, although often with morals attached, we find the Arabic version of the Sanskrit Fables of Bidpai, composed by εAbdullāh b. al-Muqaffaε (d. 760), and the Arabian Nights, various versions of which crystallized from Sanskrit and Persian models in the tenth century. Another common style was the stringing together of instruction and anecdote, as in the Book of Animals by al-Jāḥiz (d. 869), The Unique Necklace, composed in Spain by Ibn εAbdi Rabbihi (d. 940), and the Book of Songs by Abū 1-Faraj al-Isfahānī (d. 967), which uses a collection of Arabian poems set to music as the basis for an eclectic discussion of the incidents which occasioned their composition, the lives of the poets and their patrons, and the conditions of life in pre-Islamic Arabia. More edifying popularizations were written by Ibn Qutayba (d. 889), and some of his titles, set among works on history and literary criticism, state the nature of this type of belles lettres very explicitly: The Fountains of Story, The Book of Subjects of Knowledge, The Adab of the Secretary (here often translated 'culture' or 'accomplishments'). This tradition was carried into the eleventh century by Abū 1-Ḥayyān al-Tawḥīdī (d. 1023) and al-Thaεālibī (d. 1038). The secretaries themselves developed a stylistic tradition, using rhymed prose with highly self-conscious elaboration, in their letters (risāla, pl. rasā'il) especially those of Ibn al-Amīd (d. 970), al-Khawārizmī (d. 993) and al-Ṣāhib (d. 995).

The last really important stylistic innovation of Classical Arabic prose was the maqāma (often translated 'assembly'), created by Badīεu l-Zamān al-Ḥamadānī (d. 1007), and then developed by al-Ḥarīrī to one of the liveliest branches of Arabic literature. In the maqāmāt a series of vignettes are strung together, describing in rhymed prose, with every possible rhetorical device, the encounters of the narrator with a lovable ruffian who recounts his exploits. During the modern period, the maqāma has had almost as great a prestige as the qasīda, and just as modern poetry was to struggle with the effort to modernize or abandon the qasīda, the maqāma was felt to have the authority of a native Arabic literary form which might be developed into drama or into an Arab novel.

Poetry had always been the Arab art par excellence and was invaded by non-Arabs with much greater trepidation, since the philologists who had collected and studied the ancient poetry had rigidly defined the nature of poetics and the permissible subjects and styles, comparing each new work with the ancient models. The sphere of prose, however, was constantly expanded, so that poetry lost its position as the only medium with rhetorical authority; according to one tradition, prose supplanted poetry in the middle of the ninth century. Nevertheless, poetry was an essential part of court life, and it is possible to follow several tendencies in its development. There was an increasing specialization, with a greater development of love songs and wine songs (Abū Nuwās (d. 810), one of the greatest of Arabic poets, a famous member of the court of Hārūn al-Rashīd who appears in the Arabian Nights), or ascetic and ṣūfī (mystic) verse (Abū l-εAtāhiya (d. 828)). New metaphorical devices, called badīε ('innovation'), enriched all poetry, even that which remained close to the classical tradition, but was carried to extreme lengths in a branch of poetry that was decidedly

un-Arab in feeling. BadīƐ was invented by Bashshār b. Burd
(d. 783), a blind poet of Persian origin, and was adopted by a
series of poets, al-Sanawbarī, Kushājim, and ƐUqaylī, who created
ever more elaborate tropes describing wine and garden landscapes.
This poetry of refinement was in strong contrast with a slangy
form of poetry which was developing in the great towns of Meso-
potamia. However, two of the most distinguished poets of the
period, al-Mutanabbī and Abū Firās (d. 968), both of whom lived
at the glittering court of Sayfu l-Dawla in Aleppo, preferred to
go back to the classical tradition, and a later poet, known for
his free-thinking and the tortuous elaboration of his prose,
al-MaƐarrī (d. 1057), followed their precedent from a linguistic
point of view.

2.34 Arabic literature in decline

Towards the end of the ƐAbbāsid period and in the centuries that
followed, Arabic literature lost most of its vigor, lasting
slightly longer in Spain than in the East. Poetry was the earliest genre to decline, for although there were always scores of
poets ready to copy the old forms, the only creative voices were
those of the ṣūfīs and mystics who used poetry to express their
religious experiences, ƐUmar b. al-Farīd (d. 1235) and Ibn ƐArabī
(d. 1240). The adab tradition was already languishing in the
eleventh century and al-Ḥarīrī was the last great innovator in
that tradition. More serious forms of prose writing lasted
longer: ṭabaqāt of importance continued to be written (for instance, the Biographical Dictionary of Ibn Khallikān, (d. 1282),
and the work of encyclopedists such as al-Suyūṭī (d. 1505)). A
North African, Ibn Khaldūn (1332-1406), propounded a magnificent
theory of history which is explained in his Muqaddima, based on
the group cohesiveness which gives the nomads their advantage in
a cyclic struggle with dynasties following an internal law of
decay. However, he lived at a time when originality was a rare
exception.

Philosophy was one of the later forms of classical literature
to develop in Arabic, beginning with al-Kindī (d. 850) and

al-Farābī (d. 950), and continuing with Ibn Sinā [Avicenna]
(d. 1037), al-Ghazālī (d. 1111) the great reconciler of ṣūfism
and orthodoxy, and Ibn Rushd [Averroës] (d. 1198), but it could
not survive the religious rigidity of the years that followed.
Geography, which was initiated by Ibn Khurdādbih, in charge of
ᵉAbbāsid posts in the ninth century, had a rich development during which it absorbed many of the features of adab, as the wonders
of foreign lands became more intriguing than the details of desert
life, and reached a high point in the travels of Ibn Baṭṭūṭa
(d. 1377).

Although Arabic literature had started its decline two centuries before the Mongol sack of Baghdad in 1258, the effect of
the sack itself was not as drastic as might have been expected,
because the Islamic world had already long ceased to be central-
ized around a single imperial capital. During the long years of
disintegration, two areas that had been of immense importance to
Arabic literature were completely eliminated as possible sources:
Spain, when the Moors were first oppressed and then driven out,
and Persia, as the Persian language replaced Arabic and Persians
began to glorify their own pre-Islamic past. From the end of the
fifteenth century to the beginning of the modern period, the Arab
lands were ruled from Istanbul by Ottoman Turks, and these centuries were almost completely unproductive, partly due to decay
and misrule, but also in great part to the fact that membership
in the ruling class was open to those who learned Turkish and became Ottomans, so that talent from all over the empire was at-
tracted to this new imperial identity. Arabic was no longer the
only language of Islam, and the use of Arabic no longer conferred
prestige and was required only in some specifically religious
contexts where the concern was with continuity and memorization,
rather than with creativity. The story of Arabic literature
stops here and does not resume until the nineteenth century, when
the new literature begins to be Arab as well as Arabic.

2.35 Modern Arabic literature

The modern period opened for the Arabs in 1798 when Napoleon

landed in Egypt, although it took another fifty years before a
new Arab literature really began to take shape for the Arab
Renaissance (nahḍa).[1] The first steps were the efforts of
Muḥammad ʿAlī and his followers who ruled Egypt after the French
withdrawal and who had seen enough of modern Western methods to
want to train technicians in the new skills, either by sending
them to Europe or by establishing schools in Egypt. The next
generation, the children of these technicians, became intellectuals trying to define first the political-philosophical and
then the aesthetic canons of the new era, and they were supplemented by a steady stream of Syrians and Lebanese, many of whom
had been trained in Christian missionary schools established in
the second half of the nineteenth century.

Nineteenth century Arabic literature was composed of several
strands. The first was woven by journalists and essayists com-
menting on day-to-day problems and putting them in an ideological
setting. Al-Afghānī (d. 1897) and Muḥammad ʿAbduh (d. 1905) are
the most famous thinkers of the period who tried to formulate,
modernize, and purify Islam, while Muṣṭafā Kāmil (d. 1908) and
Luṭfī al-Sayyid (d. 1963) were for creating a secular Western
state. A great deal of translating was also done, both technical and literary, and drama was introduced to Arabic via
translations and early experiments in dramatic rhymed prose by
the Lebanese Naqqāsh family. At the same time, explicitly literary Arabic was still closely bound to the classical tradition:
while the essayists strained at the limits of the risāla, these
were much less confining than those of the maqāma and the qaṣīda,
which were not replaced by novel and drama or by newer poetic
forms until the beginning of the twentieth century. In poetry
the qaṣīda, which has a considerable grip to this day, was the
only area in which neoclassicism really flourished, in the work
of such poets as the Egyptians al-Bārūdī (d. 1904), Aḥmad Shawqī
(d. 1932), Ḥāfiẓ Ibrāhīm (d. 1932), ʿAlī al-Jārim (d. 1949), and
ʿAzīz Abāẓa, or the Iraqi Maʿrūf al-Ruṣāfī (d. 1945). These men
varied in the strictness with which they conformed to the classical

model, sometimes using the standard content of Bedouin poetry,
with desert camp sites and camels, and sometimes interpreting
the sequence of themes more abstractly, for instance, trans-
posing the journey theme to a modern vehicle, but they all used
the metrical forms and the lexical elaboration that characterized
the classical ode.

In the first quarter of the twentieth century, a generation
of Arab writers appeared in Egypt who were much more clearly in
favor of westernization and secularization than the previous
generation, and relied on an underlying national character, which
they visualized as going back to the Pharaohs, to preserve a
fundamentally Egyptian flavor in their writing. Many of these
writers are still living; they include Muḥammad Ḥusayn Haykal,
who wrote the first truly Arabic novels, introducing colloquial
Arabic for dialogue; Ṭāha Ḥusayn, perhaps the most famous of
modern Egyptian writers, who was also at one time minister of
education, and whose autobiography The Days has been translated
into several western languages; ɛAbbās Maḥmūd al-ɛAqqād and
ɛAbd al-Qādir al-Māzinī (d. 1949), journalist-essayists; Tawfīq
al-Ḥakīm and Maḥmūd Taymūr, who created the modern Arabic drama;
and finally Aḥmad Amīn, who set out out to write a vast social
and intellectual history of Islam. During this period, some of
the poets who were later to carry their rebellion much further
published collections of verse where, without undertaking a real
rupture with tradition, they endeavored to loosen its hold, and
eliminate the archaisms that made neoclassical poetry stiff and
artificial. The Lebanese Muṭrān Khalīl Muṭrān and the Egyptian
ɛAbd al-Raḥmān Shukrī published such collections in 1908 and
1909 respectively, still as very young men.

This period of working towards a lucid modernism ended in the
twenties[2], and perhaps its bankruptcy should be dated at the
publication in 1926 of Ṭāha Ḥusayn's famous book on pre-Islamic
poetry in which he outraged orthodoxy by suggesting that the
whole corpus of pre-Islamic poetry had been forged under Islam
by the reciters and philologists, so that, by implication, all

Qur'ānic interpretations based on its linguistic evidence were
invalid. The reaction to this suggestion was so vehement that
the book was withdrawn and later reissued with offensive passages removed. The response to the discovery of the superficial
relationship between these westernizing writers and the society
they lived in was not an attempt to return to Classical norms,
but a surge of emotionalism and subjectivity in literature and
a tendency towards reaction and xenophobia in political thought.
Ten years earlier, ɛAbd al-Raḥmān Shukrī had published for a
few brief years in a strain of exaltant, romantic self-discovery,
and now this strand was picked up in the poetry of wijdān
('emotion'), which supplanted the enlightened neoclassicism.
The poets of wijdān tended to be essayists as well, highly conscious of themselves as investigating the nature of poetic truth,
especially ɛAbbās Maḥmūd al-ɛAqqād, ɛAbd al-Qādir al-Māzinī,
Ibrāhīm Nājī (d. 1953), and Abū l-Qāsim al-Shābbī (d. 1934).
Although it was short-lived, the journal Apollo, published in
Cairo from 1932 to 1934 and almost completely written by Aḥmad
Zakī Abū Shādī, was a pivotal influence in the search for 'pure
poetry' and the abandonment of all the classical prosodic forms.

After World War II, Beirut became increasingly important as a
literary and intellectual center. This was partly due to the
fact that the work of emigré writers, the writers of the Mahjar
in America, who were able, living outside the Arab world, to make
radical experiments in form while continuing to write in Arabic,
had begun to be reabsorbed. Lebanese writers of importance include Faraḥ Anṭūn, Amīn al-Rayḥānī (d. 1940), Mīkhā'īl Nuɛayma,
Muṭrān Khalīl Muṭrān and Jubrān Khalīl Jubrān. This last poet
is well known for his English writings as well, where his name
takes the form Khalil Gibran (The Prophet, etc.), and the prose
poem which he used so effectively became, with free verse, one
of the vehicles used by this generation.

By the late fifties and early sixties, Arabic literature began to lose this quality of revolution and counter-revolution.
Older writers are conscious of how far their positions have moved,

while younger ones see the old battle lines as blurred and are
more concerned with expressing themselves as individuals and
experimenting with types of symbolism rather than with linguistic
forms, since the predominance of free verse exemplifies the con-
summation of formal experimentation. The linguistic problems
that remain are those faced by the whole community, namely,
the fact that however far experiments with written Arabic are
taken, it is still not the normal spoken language of any part of
the Arab world. Contemporary essayists have developed a mature
style and contemporary poets find obscurities of thought as
attractive as obscurities of diction were once burdensome. The
greatest problems are faced by novelists and dramatists who must
make the formal idiom as natural and true to life as they can,
and they must work this out in relation to television, radio,
and moving pictures, which are becoming more and more important.
However, the modern Arab novel, in the hands of such writers as
Ṣuhayl Idrīs of Lebanon and Najīb Maḥfūẓ of Egypt, has by now
come of age.

There are many young Arabs writing now in all the Arab countries so that it is not possible to point to a single center or
to list half a dozen names. Two important trends can be mentioned in addition to the trend towards symbolism described above:
the appearance of a number of important women writers (Nāzik
al-Malā'ika, an Iraqi poetess, and Layla Baɛalbakī, a Lebanese
novelist, author of I Live, are two examples), and the increase
in short stories, many of them describing the life of villagers
or slum dwellers. Arabic has come to be a language in which the
role of the writer and the different literary genres open to him
are quite closely comparable to the literary roles and genres of
European literature. No longer is· he a tribal functionary, no
longer is his every use of the language interwoven with the
religious-philological tradition, or made the means of induct-
ing non-Arabs into a civilization. Arabs write today as individuals with greater or lesser degrees of religious or social
engagement, essentially seeking their own best self-expression

in the next best thing to a mother tongue. The fact that the language they write is not their mother tongue is part of a complex situation which will be described in Chapter 3.

2.4 The influence of Arabic on other languages

Before discussing the actual use of Classical Arabic in the Arab lands today, it is necessary to give some indication of the influence of Arabic on a number of other languages in areas where Classical Arabic is not now the standard written language.

The areas where Arabic triumphed were primarily those where some form of Semitic was already in use; the interaction of Arabic with these other forms is part of the problem of the colloquials, and will be dealt with in the next chapter. In areas where non-Semitic languages were in use (especially Berber in North Africa, Indo-Iranian in Persia and India, and Turkic in Asia Minor, the Caucasus, and Central Asia), the original languages survived, but the conversion of their speakers to Islam had drastic effects. Arabic is one of the major languages of civilization, like Latin or Chinese, with a pervasive effect in the areas of its influence throughout the Islamic world. This effect was linked to the fact that the linguistic style of the Qur'ān and Muhammad's use of Arabic were considered necessary and intrinsic parts of revelation, so that the Qur'ān could not, in orthodox Islam, be translated, read, or recited in any other language. To this day, pious Muslims from Indonesia to the Sahara know lengthy portions of Arabic by heart although they may have no active control of the language, may drastically distort the phonology, and have a varying comprehension of what they are saying. Furthermore, the technical vocabulary of the new religion, some of it Qur'ānic and some of it coined to describe increasing institutionalization, entered the lexicon of the converted peoples. Since Islam influences every sphere of life and law, this has meant that vast numbers of Arabic loanwords entered other languages, including most of the words referring to the apparatus of government.

ARABIC AND OTHER LANGUAGES

The adoption of the Arabic alphabet, because it was so much more appropriate to Arabic morphological forms, tended to reinforce these borrowings, both by making them easier to read and by dramatizing the relationships between words derived from the same root. As usual with linguistic borrowing, the vast majority of the loans were noun forms but these included verbal nouns and participles from the derived forms, so that the recognition of roots was important. A number of particles were also borrowed.

In addition, it is clear from an examination of the figures who created Arabic literature that during the period when Islam was united, a knowledge of Arabic was necessary for any scholarly or political advancement—Arabic was an imperial language—and ambitious and talented men of all national backgrounds used Arabic as their medium for all kinds of written expression. Those who could not write pure Arabic did their best and those who could not really write Arabic at all wrote their own languages with as many Arabic loans as possible. When Arabic ceased to be the imperial language, nations with an old tradition of civilization, especially Persia, used their own languages except when dealing with specifically religious subjects, but the vast number of loanwords and the alphabet that fostered them were retained. Nations Islamized after the decline of the caliphate often looked to Persia as a center of civilization, but in borrowing from Persia they took at least as much Arabic as Persian. Up to the nineteenth century, it was virtually possible, with a knowledge of Arabic and the Arabic alphabet, to read Ottoman Turkish, Persian, and Urdu. Writers in these languages included the whole lexicon of Arabic for possible use and treated most Arabic forms according to the grammatical rules of their source.

Modern nationalistic movements and the decline in religious and classical education have affected these loans to varying degrees. The Turks of modern Turkey have abandoned the Arabic alphabet of Ottoman, do not teach Arabic in the schools, and have made a conscious effort to purge the language of Arabic and

Persian loans. Urdu in Pakistan and Persian in Iran are still written in the old alphabet and still show many loans, but the borrowings are no longer free and even these Islamic languages have less and less in common. In areas of Africa where Islam is still spreading, Arabic moves with it as a language of civilization, and the old process tends to be partially repeated.

NOTES

1. I am indebted for much of this analysis of the modern period to the unpublished thesis of Jaroslav Stetkewycz, Modern Arabic Poetic and Prose Language (Harvard Univ., 1963).

2. Nadav Safran, Egypt in Search of Political Community: An Analysis of the Intellectual and Political Evolution of Egypt, 1804-1952 (Harvard University Press, 1961) p. 165.

3. THE LINGUISTIC PRACTICE OF THE ARABS

3.1 Speech and writing in Classical Arabic

The preceding chapter has dealt with Arabic in relation to the
other Semitic languages and with the external development of
Arabic as a literary language up to the present, and the complex
influences that it has had on the languages with which it has
been in contact. The discussion so far has been an idealized
history of only one of many dialects of Arabic, the one called
εArabīya, omitting the development of the other dialects, the
extent of their actual use, and the effect of these dialects and
of other languages on the εArabīya. εArabīya is the Arabic term
for what European writers call Classical, Written, or Literary
Arabic; these terms are sometimes used in a more specialized way,
whereby Classical Arabic refers to the language of the pre-
Islamic poets (also called the poetic koine), Literary Arabic
refers to the prose language of medieval Islam, and the modern
uses are referred to as Modern Standard Arabic.

3.11 The origins of Classical Arabic

Pre-Islamic Arabia, like present-day Saudi Arabia, included
pockets of urban and oasis settlement, often relatively pros-
perous stops on trade routes, and vast areas whose only population was nomadic. Communications were poor and there was no
central administration, but at the same time there was a con-
tinual slow shuffling of population, with some degree of communication maintained over long periods of time and great distances.
In this situation there was much dialect variation, although it
is difficult to mark the boundaries of any particular dialect.
The Arab grammarians recognized these dialect variations, referring to them to explain unusual forms and generally classifying them to reflect the tribal rivalries of their own period.
Two large groupings of dialects have been identified[1] the Western
group, spoken in the mountainous strip that parallels the western

coast of Arabia and the relatively fertile land lying between it
and the coast and in another area on the Persian Gulf, and the
Eastern group spoken in the remainder of the peninsula (except
in those areas where South Arabic, a distinct language, was
spoken; see 2.1). Western Arabic was spoken in Yemen and in the
Ḥijāz, the area where Islam developed in the Holy Cities of Mecca
and Medina. Eastern Arabic was the language of the important
tribes of Tamīm, Rabīᵋa, Asad, and others of the Qays confederation, and was the dominant strain, in spite of heavy Western
influences, in the Najd (the central area of the peninsula, to
the northeast of the Ḥijāz); significantly, this is the area
where the major experiments in political organization, the
evanescent empire of Kinda and the Qays confederation, took
place, and where Arabic poetry is said to have evolved (Imru'u
l-Qays, for instance, was a hereditary prince of Kinda). ᵋArabīya
or Classical Arabic seems to have developed in the Najd, combining features of several different dialects into a common language
which was used for some kinds of intertribal communication.
Phonologically, it resembles the Western dialects, which had a
full vowel system, relatively little consonant assimilation, and
two phonemes corresponding to /ā/ which are reflected in the two
ways of spelling final /ā/ in ClA. On the other hand, the hamza
/ʔ/ tended to be lost in the Western dialects, whereas the Eastern dialects preserved it, sometimes exaggerating it to /ɛ/; ClA
preserves the hamza and resembles the Eastern dialects grammatically, so that it is probable that ClA is primarily Eastern,
but that it developed quite early, before the most drastic phonetic alterations had occurred in the Eastern dialects. On the
other hand, many of the Old Arabic inscriptions seem to be pre-
dominantly Western, and are certainly not direct ancestors of
ClA. Western Arabic is of special interest because many of its
grammatical features identify it as a link with Northwest Semitic.

Classical Arabic was associated with a particular type of
poetry and was spread along with that poetic tradition to all
parts of Arabia; it seems never to have been identical with any

normal spoken dialect, so that it was necessary for poets to be trained in its use, but of course it was much more different from the dialects of Mecca and Medina than it was from the dialects of the Najd where it developed. Illiterate Bedouin tribes do not now use this dialect for poetic composition, but they do seem to have used it for several centuries after Islam, so that they remained useful informants for the philologists, and it is still true that in many areas oral poetry is composed in a different dialect from the dialect of normal speech, borrowing from a nearby or more Bedouin group or preserving archaic features[2]. It was associated with solemn or eloquent speech and was useful currency for intertribal communication, so it is not surprising that it was the appropriate medium for the Qur'ān. The various traditions of recitation and anomalous orthographic features of the Qur'ān remain a valuable source of information about Western Arabic.

The use of the poetic dialect, which is often referred to as a poetic koine (by analogy with Greek) because of its intertribal character, was reinforced as the Islamic community became increasingly mixed, commanding a supertribal loyalty. Although early writers seem to reflect a knowledge of the dialectal mixture in Arabia and the fact that the idiom of the Qur'ān was not that of the Quraysh tribe to which the Prophet belonged, Muslims of later centuries came to believe that the ɛArabīya was the normal speech of nomadic Arabia, that it had reached its fullest perfection in Quraysh, and that all deviations from it were corruptions. As the result of the labors of the philologists, the poetic dialect was codified to the point where it became a much more homogeneous language than it had ever been in the mouths of the pre-Islamic poets. The grammatical rules reflect a knowledge of a standard separate from the Qur'ān, and the original mixture of dialects is reflected in the great lexical richness of Classical Arabic.

3.12 Classical Arabic in the Islamic Empire

Classical Arabic must really be considered to date from the moment when the Islamic administration and the maintenance of religious orthodoxy put a premium on the use of a single, standardized, and

unifying dialect. Classical Arabic represents the ancient poetic
koine frozen at a particular moment of its existence, whereas it
must once have been relatively fluid—such a fluid state is reflected in the dīwān, or tribal anthology, of the Hudhayl tribe,
collected in the early Islamic period, which shows considerable
deviation from the Classical norm. Even more deviant forms, of
which Muḥammad's own is one example (although most of these have
tended to be normalized wherever they were written down), must
have been used by those who were not professional poets, but took
advantage of the intertribal dialect for trade and politics.
Within less than a century, the love poetry written in the Ḥijāz
(see 2.32) reflected radical changes in style and some linguistic
change, which can only partly be attributed to non-Arab elements
of the population.

Nevertheless, a real effort was made to maintain Classical
Arabic as the language of the court[3]. This was always a self-
conscious process, which included a great deal of discussion of
the correct forms, and was made possible by continually drawing
on Bedouins, especially rāwīs, the professional reciters of
poetry who were trained in the poetic koine, and by sending
young men to visit in Bedouin tribes. 'Puristic' anecdotes
date from the end of the seventh century. It seems to have been
extremely difficult, however, to maintain this dual tradition
and by the ninth century almost no effort was made to use iɛrāb
('Bedouin' speech with full inflectional endings) in conversation. The standard of mastery of Classical Arabic seems to
have steadily declined, lasting only slightly longer in the
centers of culture and administration than it did in the tribal
areas, until it became the preserve of experts—the grammarians
who made a lifelong study of it and trained their own students
to carry on their traditions. The lapse of Classical Arabic
from spoken use probably corresponds quite closely to the point
where it became fully a written language—where illiterates no
longer mastered it and the norm was set by written style to
which formal speech might make an effort to conform. As the

Arab empire declined, first Persian and then Turkish edged Classical Arabic out of more and more areas of use and forced it to
become more and more specialized.

A comparison with the preceding chapter will show that the
great body of Arabic literature was produced after the spoken use
of the language began to decline and that much of it was addressed
to just this problem. The procedure was a cumbersome one, however;
there was never a very large group of men with sufficient training
to produce literature, and during a period of massive cultural
decline the rigors of training in Classical Arabic tended to limit
it to pedants and its use to specifically religious scholarship.

3.13 The modern use of Classical Arabic

Whereas during the pre-Islamic period the spoken dialects were
primarily tribal, they became regional and now have an increasing tendency to be national. Classical Arabic has always had a
number of special contexts which demanded its use, has required
some degree of special training in a language different from the
language of childhood and family life which was only acquired by
a portion of the population, and has carried with it prestige and
access to the richest portions of the culture. The modern Arab
world represents a continuation of this situation, which has been
called diglossia[4]. The other face of diglossia, namely the nature
and distribution of the vernaculars, will be explored below (see
3.2).

Classical Arabic in its secular use is now an international
language; in the modern Middle East, it is the language which
Iraq, Syria, Jordan, Egypt, Lebanon, Tunisia, Libya, the Sudan,
Morocco, Algeria, Saudi Arabia, Yemen, Kuwait, Aden, etc., have
in common. It has been adopted by all of these countries as an
official language and is the only form of Arabic which achieves
full official recognition. Its importance goes even further than
this, for it is the chief symbol of ethnic unity among the Arabs
and is essential to any kind of Pan-Arabism. Any attempt to resolve the problems of diglossia by moving towards a more extensive use of the regional dialects runs into the impassioned

79

opposition of those who see ClA as the essential basis for the
common Arab nation; an Arab is defined as anyone who 'speaks
Arabic and thinks of himself as an Arab', and this is a definition which is only meaningful if it is taken, ideally, as referring to ClA, since the regional dialects are not all mutually
intelligible. Arabs who cannot use ClA to some degree may have
to fall back on English or French (if they know these languages;
see 3.3) if they come from widely separated regions. Therefore,
ClA still possesses that vital element which was the basis for
its adoption as the language of the Islamic umma ('community'):
it is a unifying factor, nowadays crossing the borders of different political systems, different economic environments,
widely varying cultures and physical types, and different reli-
gions. It is also international in the sense that it is the
form of Arabic which is most used in international contact with
non-Arab nations: the BBC transmits broadcasts in ClA and international treaties and agreements with Arab nations have versions
in ClA.

Classical Arabic is also international in its religious and
liturgical use and in religious courts as the language of Islam.
The Qur'ān may be discussed in colloquial or in other Muslim languages like Urdu, but it is normally read in ClA. Translations
have generally been regarded as invalid and limited to marginal
groups like the Ahmadīya and the Black Muslims in the United
States, and this may well remain true for Islam as an international religion. In this context, the ɛArabīya embraces an
even wider sphere and becomes of paramount value to theologians
who cherish the unity of Islam.

Classical Arabic still retains the connotation which it had
as a poetic koine of being more beautiful and more significant—
indeed, this is often carried to the point where the elegant
expression of an idea may be taken as evidence of its validity.
ClA is the language in which important things are said, in ad-
dressing God, in crossing national boundaries, and in science
and the arts. The same emphasis on form that is so apparent in

the historical development of Arabic literature has its counter-
part today in a lingering tendency to judge what is said by the
way in which it is said. Furthermore, many Arabs take pleasure
in listening to ClA even when they are unable to understand the
content and may write long passages of eloquent double-talk for
the pleasure of the language, which are read with little awareness that the information conveyed is minimal. The inflectional
grammar of the written language is regarded as a work of art,
whereas Arabs are often unwilling to recognize that the dialects
have any grammar, but see them as chaotic deviations from the
sacred norm. Educated Arabs feel very strongly about grammatical correctness and will almost always find fault with a passage
they are asked to correct—and often, too, when they are not
asked. The feeling that Arabic grammar embodies a high and difficult truth is expressed in a general scepticism about the
possibility of any non-Arab ever 'really' learning Arabic. This
may be very discouraging to students, especially if they do not
realize that the modern educated Arab, unless he is a specialist,
is himself far from being at home in Classical poetry and prose,
and is very often at a loss for the correct inflectional form.
Since ClA is the only form of the language which is normally
written, it is pragmatically the only way of access (except for
European languages) to any form of education or culture or to
any participation in the national life outside the local scene.
All books and newspapers are in Classical Arabic, all translations from European languages are into ClA, and all formal instruction is in ClA. Most radio broadcasting is in the classical language, as are almost all political speeches. All correspondence takes place in the only form of Arabic that can be
written and in theory all bureaucratic functions depend on it.

It is worth pointing out that in most of these contexts the
level of correctness achieved may be quite low. Radio broadcasts may be understood by those who could not begin to approximate them, and most Arabs, when they are dealing with printed
material, do not maintain an awareness of the grammatical

81

functions which would be necessary in order to read it out loud
correctly—they seem to read the consonantal skeleton and to get
enough information from it to understand the grammatical construction without being able to achieve a full vocalization.
They may write the same way, and it is a feature of modern
Arabic style that it is relatively hospitable to this approach.
Furthermore, while Classical Arabic is used in formal instruction and prepared lectures, discussion slips readily into modified forms of Colloquial. Similarly, government officials may
discuss written material which is in front of them in Colloquial.
However, all this takes place in contexts where the initial tone
is set and the basic material provided by the written language,
so that although academic and intellectual subjects may be discussed in the dialects, ClA provides the framework for the discussion, and participation is hardly possible for the fully
illiterate. A model for this may be found in dealing with literature written in the dialects: in many parts of the Arab world,
aside from the use of passages of colloquial dialogue, songs and
folklore have been collected in dialect and conventions adopted
for writing these in the Arabic alphabet. However, these written
forms of Colloquial Arabic are normally used only by those who
have arrived at literacy via the classical language itself.

In the modern renaissance, the sphere of Classical Arabic has
been greatly expanded, not so much because of a change in the
nature of the situation of diglossia, but because the new spheres
of life in which Arabic is used in the twentieth century tend to
fall into the categories governed by Classical: the use of the
radio and the introduction of drama fall in this category, and so
does most advertising and propaganda. Furthermore, the importance
of science is radically increased and ClA has been stretched to
accommodate new concepts and vocabularies (see 3.142), just as it
has been challenged to meet new art forms. This is in contrast
to the relatively more stable nature of the areas of colloquial
expression in rural areas and in family and other informal conversation. Much of the terminology which deals with political

and technological conditions is borrowed into Colloquial either from Classical or from European languages, with Classical playing the more important role. What this means is that the confrontation with the twentieth century has tended to take place in ClA because it is international, because it is 'eloquent' and 'significant', and because it is written. Not only is it the Arab's only entry to his cultural resources in the past and in other parts of the Arab world, it is his primary entry into the future.

Unfortunately, the medieval situation is still reflected in the fact that ClA remains the possession of an elite. All of the Arab countries are engaged, to varying degrees, in fighting illiteracy, since the spread of the ability to read is not only practically necessary for the smooth functioning of a modern society, but has a heavy ideological load. Those who cannot read are in many ways disinherited, and in the Arab countries they face special obstacles because they must acquire a new language in order to learn. This leads to the suggestion that the only way of 'democratizing' Arabic is to write the vernaculars in a modernized script, so that literacy will depend simply on the mastery of a rational script for writing the generally spoken language; in the Soviet Union, for instance, several modified Cyrillic alphabets have been developed for writing the Arabic dialects spoken by groups of Arabic speakers in Central Asia (the residue of the furthest wave of conquests), effectively democratizing the language and at the same time fragmenting these groups and cutting them off from Arab nationalism and a share in the old and new cultural wealth of the Arab world.

Diglossia deepens the plight of the illiterate because it means that he may be unable to understand news broadcasts and political speeches along with his inability to grasp these in their written form. It also makes illiteracy much more difficult to combat and complicates primary education. Fifteen years ago, adult illiteracy (by even the most rudimentary definition of literacy) ranged between 85% and 90% throughout North Africa and in Iraq, went higher than 95% in Saudi Arabia and the other

political units of the Arabian Peninsula, with slightly better
rates in the Fertile Crescent: 70-75% in Jordan and 50-55% in
Lebanon.[5] The rate was everywhere highest for women and in rural
areas. Since that time, all of the countries have legislated
universal, free elementary education through the sixth year, but
none of the Arab countries has actually succeeded in registering
all children (especially girls) in elementary schools; the programs usually omit nomadic population (as do literacy figures
in the census), and are seriously deficient in rural areas. Programs to spread literacy among the adult population have been
rather limited.

3.14 The modern form of Classical Arabic[6]

Although Classical Arabic has been extensively studied, focussing
on the norms established by the grammarians or on the language of
specific literature, especially the Qur'ān, Arabs and westerners
have tended to assume that all written Arabic was essentially the
same, reflecting various degrees of purity or affectation. This
doctrine has been the basis of most teaching, and it is true that
the structural sketch in Chapter 1 is applicable to all written
Arabic, from the Qur'ān to tomorrow's newspapers in Cairo or
Damascus. However, several important kinds of change are taking
place which are leading to an extensive differentiation of 'Modern
Standard Arabic'.

(1) There exist a series of 'acceptable' simplifications in
    realizing ClA, and there are a number of overlapping ways in
    which ClA is influenced by the dialects or accommodates to
    them.

(2) There is a vast shift in the lexicon, due to the need for
    technical terminology, which remains a critical problem in
    the Arab world; this sometimes has grammatical implications.
    In this context, the general nature of the Arabic lexicon
    may be summed up.

(3) There are a number of stylistic changes due to translations
    from European languages and extensive bilingualism.
    These changes are, in general, due either to the spread of

literacy or to the diffusion of European culture and seem to be
signs of vitality in the language, which may or may not be able
to unfold sufficiently rapidly to meet the need.

3.141 Simplifications and Colloquial influences

Most simplifications that are acceptable in writing are based on
a limitation in the range of forms—the omission of syntactic
structures used by classical authors and a drastic reduction in
vocabulary. There is some tolerance for vagueness in, for instance, the exact reference of pronouns or the choice of the
appropriate tense in conditional sentences. In general, modern
written Arabic accommodates to the dialects by the selection of
forms that are not dependent on short vowels for their understanding, whereas 'classicizing' and the search for a loftier
style take place in the lexical range, sometimes by the selection,
where ClA offers two forms, of the less colloquial, e.g. the use
of /hīna/ 'when' instead of /lamma/, which also appears in the
dialects. Many particles have undergone a slight shift in meaning /hattā/ 'until' often means 'even', and /ʔidā/ 'when' means
'if'. Particles play an increasingly important role in the
sentence, defining tenses more precisely (/sawfa/ + imperfect for
the future), and expressing relationships which might be expressed
by the construct (such constructions usually use the Classical
/bi-/, /min/, etc., but in the Syrian area /tābiɛ/ 'according to,
pertaining to' [ClA 'following'] is very common: /lajnatu
lmuwāṣalāti ddāʔimatu ttābiɛatu lilʔamānati lɛammati lijāmiɛati
dduwali lɛarabīyah/ 'the Permanent Commission on Communications
of the Secretary General of the Arab League') and indicating in-
definiteness: /baytun/ > /ʔahadu lbuyūt/. One example of an
analogical extension is the occasional use of /-ūn/ for adjectives modifying plurals of rational masculine beings, even where
a broken plural exists, e.g. /kabīr/ 'big' appears with the plural
/kabīrūn/ instead of /kibār/ by analogy with participles and adjectives with suffixed /-īy/. A few feminine superlatives are
used simply as adjectives, appearing in both definite and indefinite: /šarikatun kubrā/ 'a big company'.

There is a further group of forms which are not reflected in
the writing but are strictly errors in the pronunciation of ClA
and yet are tolerated. Spoken ClA is sufficiently influenced by
colloquial pronunciation and idiom so that it is almost always
possible to tell where a broadcast originates; the Egyptian
radio[7] (which is most notorious for this) maintains the [g] pronunciation of the Classical /j/ and follows the Colloquial stress
patterns, since stress is generally a regional feature and not
really part of the ClA system. ClA /t̲/, /d̲/, and /z̲/ (=[d̲])
have become dentals /t/, /d/, /ḍ/ in most urban dialects, and
where speakers cannot produce interdentals, [s], [z], and [z̲]
are accepted. For all practical purposes, the number system
described in 1.33 does not exist in the oral use of ClA—the
short vowel patterns are a myth and the speaker uses the simplified forms current in his own dialect for numbers above ten,
even though he may be able to write the correct consonantal
skeleton. Most important, the ClA convention for omitting short
vowel endings in pause (see 1.24) gives the Arab an escape route,
for by breaking his sentence into shorter segments he may legit-
imately omit many of the grammatical endings which discomfit him.
In slovenly speech which would not be acceptable on the radio,
all forms may be in pause, except where the following word begins with a consonant cluster, especially in construct, and here
a colorless vowel may be supplied. The contrast of pause vs.
context has become much more flexible than it was and Arabs vary
in their pronunciation of feminine nouns in pause (/-ah/, /-at/,
or /-a/), of the adjective suffix (/-ī/ or /-īy/) and of indefinite masculine accusatives (traditionally /-ā/, now normally
/-an/).

3.142 Lexical development

The historical Arabic lexicon includes vast numbers of words from
different areas and epochs. Since all the accumulated nuances of
these words have been preserved with them, meanings in context
are often difficult to determine. When dictionaries of synonyms
were written, words for 'camel' or 'sword', 'rain' or 'lion'

stretched into long lists; side by side with these, dictionaries
of special vocabulary dealt with the highly specialized terms
developed in nomadic Arabia for plants or topographical features
or points of the camel's anatomy. Every Arabic word is said to
have four meanings: its primary meaning—the precise opposite—
something obscene—something to do with a camel! In practice,
only a small portion of this vast accumulated vocabulary is used,
except for conscious and conspicuous archaism, and words listed
in traditional dictionaries with half a dozen very different meanings are now generally limited to one or two. Outside of the portion in general use, the ancient vocabulary provides a treasury of
words which may be analogically reinterpreted to fit modern contexts: two relatively rare words for caravan, /qiṭār/ and /say.
yarāh/, are now in use for 'train' and 'automobile', respectively.
Modern biologists sometimes reapply to specific forms of flora
and fauna words whose precise ancient meanings are unknown.

Although the various linguistic academies in the Arab world
sympathize with this technique, it is relatively cumbersome for
purposeful use, because the fact that a word is already in existence in an obscure dictionary does not absolve modern users of
the necessity of learning it in its modern definition and there
is a certain amount of negative feedback. On the other hand, it
is one of the chief methods of vocabulary development in a natural
evolution. It has been especially important as Arabic has borrowed specialized usages of words which were originally Arabic
but were borrowed by Persian and then Turkish; many modern administrative terms fall into this category.

The Arabic lexicon is structured by the various patterns for
derivation of nouns and verbs from existing roots, and all dictionaries are organized around these roots. The relationship
between meaning and pattern is, as has been pointed out, rather
vague and subject to semantic shift over long periods of time,
but where patterns are still open (e.g. muCāCaCah is still open
to new coinages as a verbal noun for Form III verbs, whereas
CiCāC, which sometimes occurs, is not; similarly, the derivation

of quadriliteral roots by adding a fourth consonant between C_1 and C_3, the $?aC_1C_2aC_3{\sim}C_1aC_2C_3\bar{a}?$ adjectives for color and physical defects, and verbs of Forms IX and XI, and the others omitted in this treatment, are not) words may be coined quite freely, and if they are new coinages, there is some chance of guessing their meaning. Relatively few patterns are so open that they are free- ly innovated, but most patterns are available for the invention of technical terms:

<u>Verbal nouns</u>: /ta?mīn/ 'insurance', /taᵋyīn/ 'ionization',
   /?idāᵋah/ 'broadcasting'

<u>Participles</u>: /mu?tamar/ 'conference', /mantūjāt/ 'products'

<u>Nouns of place</u>: /maṣnaᵋ/ 'factory', /mustašfā/ 'hospital',
   /maṭār/ 'airport'

It will be clear on consideration that these words represent a type of derivation which is radically different from that which occurs in Indo-European, especially in Latin and Greek, which are the reservoirs from which many European languages draw most of their technical vocabulary. First, because many technical terms are in part recognizable in English as such, e.g. we do not have to be told that 'television' means something more specific than the way the world looks from the top of a high hill; second, because English is one of a community of languages which share a technical vocabulary; and third, because (in very general terms) the Arabic system of derivation allows the Arab to com- bine only a single specific root, only one directly referential element, with a variety of modal specifications (gender, number, reference of the word to a place, a profession, a tool, a pro- cess, etc.). In coining a translation for 'television', Arabic would be constrained to choose between the reference to 'vision' and the reference to distance 'tele-'. The ideal system from the point of view of efficiency would (a) have a one-to-one correspondence, so the coinage could be automatic, and (b) would result in <u>single</u> words free to form syntactic combinations. These two features are virtually impossible to obtain without doing violence to the structure of Arabic.

In dealing with the suffixes and prefixes of Indo-European derivation, which do not have concrete references but have a semantic value (sub-, non-, semi-, post-; -like, -less, etc.) of the sort which generally occurs in particles in Arabic, the Arabs have tended to use their particles to form compounds which may only deviate from Arabic grammar when they are treated as unitary expressions—as words: /šibhu jazīrah/ 'peninsula', /ġayr qānūnīy/ 'illegal', /didda jāsūsīyah/ 'counterespionage', /lā silkīyah/ 'wireless, radio'. These forms only show their strangeness in Arabic when they are used in context as single words, like the words they translate, but this procedure leads in turn to the treatment of Arabic phrases as single words as expressed in the addition of suffixes: /lā ʔadrī/ 'I don't know' becomes /lā ʔadrīyah/ 'agnosticism' or 'I don't know-ism'. Even this deviation from the spirit of the language is limited; 'semi-agnosticism' would be hard to express in a single word in Arabic!

ClA has also expanded the use of some of its modal affixes to translate technical terms, for instance the use of /-īyah/ to produce abstract nouns such as /marksīyah/ 'Marxism', /mašrūɛīyah/ 'legitimacy', and /lā nihāʔīyah/ 'infinity'. Other modal affixes have been invented which, although they may be new, are not un-like existing morphemes. The chemist's suffixes -ate and -ite are simply taken over: /laban/ + /-āt/ → /labanāt/ 'lactate' /kibrīt/ + /-īt/ → /kibrītīt/ 'sulfite'.

In the vast majority of cases, where translating requires two referential components, the attempt to produce a translation which preserves a one-to-one correspondence with the European technical term produces a phrase which cannot be used as a word: Noun + Adjective: /ḥukmun dātīy/ 'autonomy'; Noun + Noun (in construct): /farṭu lḥāssīyah/ 'hypertension'; or, even more complex, Noun + Preposition + Noun: /qābilun lissuknah/ 'habitable, receptive to habitation'. On the other hand, the attempt to produce a single word does violence to the structure of the language, and such violence tends to be chaotic, so that many possible forms might result: /sarmanah/ from /ssayru fī lmanām/ 'going in sleep' and

/nawmašah/ from /lmašyu fī nnawm/ 'walking in sleep' have both
been coined for 'somnambulism'. Other examples of equal violence
are /balmah/ 'dehydrate', a verb from /bilā māʔ/ 'without water',
and /mutašājih/ 'isotope', an active participle from /tašābuhu
jihah/ 'similarity of aspect', but these have the advantage that
the violence has been done, in effect, at the root level, a process which is not without precedent (see 1.53), and they fit
perfectly smoothly into the Arabic sentence[8]. It is in this
category, where the choice is between a totally arbitrary translation (/raʔīs/ 'president' reflects only the meaning [or rather
the use] but not the etymology or structure of the English word),
the invention of a compound root, or the use of a phrase that
will continually require recasting sentences, that the greatest
lexical crisis exists, since the vast body of Western scientific
terminology has this form, and all coinages of single words must
be taught and cannot be recognized, while coinages of phrases are
unstable.

To the reinterpretation and revival of old terms and the derivation of new ones by more or less orthodox means may be added a
third source of new vocabulary, namely, direct borrowing from
European languages. At all periods in its history, there have
been borrowings into Arabic primarily from Indo-European and
Semitic languages, and a number of loanwords have been recognized
in the Qur'ān. Many Greek loans came into Arabic in the Middle
Ages for the adaptation of the Greek sciences, and unlike earlier
loans which fit relatively well into the Arabic phonological pattern (/ṣirāt/ 'path' from Latin strata), only a few of these
could be fully assimilated (/falsaf/ 'philosophize') while the
majority are painfully obvious (/jūgrāfīyah/ 'geography'). Such
terms are somewhat difficult to manipulate in Arabic because only
a few derivational processes can be applied to them, and it has
been felt that they blemish Arabic style. In the modern period,
nationalism has reinforced the resistance to such borrowings from
European languages, and they tend to be regarded as a last resort.
However, many words have been accepted completely and resist all

efforts to replace them; /tilifūn/, for instance, has outlived more than a dozen suggested alternatives.

Modern borrowings from European languages include a number of Italian words, many English words (/kuktīl/, /faytamīn/ and /fūlklūr/—note that this last is based on English spelling, not pronunciation), and the greatest influx of all, French words (/bitrūl/ 'petrol, gasoline'; /bilāj/ 'beach', Fr. plage, /lhayātu lbūhīmīyah/ 'la vie de bohème', and /sīnamā/). Arabs are often urged, when adopting European terms derived from the Greek, to adopt a form based on the original Greek rather than its modern form, but this is often ignored. Arabs vary in the degree to which they pronounce loanwords in accordance with the phonology of the source language, and it is necessary to distinguish between European words used by Arabs in conversation, where both speakers may be bilingual, moving freely between the two languages and drawing on the second to fill any gaps in the first, and words which have been fully assimilated into Arabic, i.e. reshaped to an acceptable phonological form as reflected in a uniform spelling. Assimilated loans are very easily supplied with adjective endings (/sīnamāʔīy/ 'cinematic') and may be considered fully acclimatized when they are assigned a regular broken plural: /kakātīl/ 'cocktails', or /ʔaflām/, plural of /film/~/filim/.

3.143 European influences on style and syntax

In addition to the European influences that affect the lexicon, and which may be necessary for the development of a vocabulary for the discussion of modern life, European languages have also had a far-reaching effect on Arabic style because the modern Arab intellectual constantly moves back and forth between Arabic and French or English, and a great part of his Arabic reading is in translations, often carelessly and mechanically done. These influences are of two kinds: direct calques (component by component translations of phrases or idioms), and distributional changes, whereby constructions parallel or similar to those of French or English are favored, resulting in a slow shift of style.

Calques appear in such phrases as /lḥarbu lbāridah/ 'the cold war', /barīṭāniyā lεuẓmā/ 'Great Britain', /qatala lwaqt/ 'kill time', /laεiba dawran/ 'play a role', /ʔaxada jiddīyan/ 'take seriously'. These are relatively obvious, but many others enter the language more subtly, appearing even in the works of stylists like Ṭaha Ḥusayn. Such calques are /qutila εalā yadi lfiransīyīn/ 'he was killed at the hand of the French', which not only includes a calqued idiom, but also the mention of the agent of a passive verb, which is normally forbidden by Arabic grammar; /kam huwa qarīb/ 'how close he is!' instead of the normal /mā ʔaqrabahu/, a special development of the elative; the use of /li-/ with verbs meaning 'to give' and /ʔilā/ with verbs of motion which take direct objects in literary Arabic; translation of 'there is, there are' by /hunāka/ or /hunālika/, which correctly only trans-late the 'there' in 'over there': /laysa hunāka ʔamalun fī.../ 'there is no hope that...' Even more subtle is the increasing frequency of such phrases as /ʔamwālu wamumtalakātu ššarikati/ 'the goods and properties of the company', instead of /ʔamwālu ššarikati wamumtalakātuhā/ 'the goods of the company and its properties', or /ʔusaʔilu nafsī/ 'I ask myself', instead of us-ing a reflexive verb.

Distributional changes seem to result from the heavy volume of literal translations, which select among the available con-structions of Arabic those constructions which parallel the original. The hack translator translates verbs into verbs and nouns into nouns, and in so doing he increases the ratio of nouns to verbs. He translates adverbs into adverbials, using the two available processes of ClA: accusative complements (/tadrījīyan/ 'gradually', /jiddīyan/ 'seriously') and prepo-sitional phrases (/bittafṣīl/ 'in detail', /birifq/ 'tenderly'). He is continually involved in the effort to maintain the oblig-atory grammatical categories of the source language and so goes out of the way to specify time or nondetermination. He is re-peatedly faced with phrases that have no perfect equivalent in Arabic, so he picks one which is approximately equivalent, and

ends up using it so heavily that it is distorted (/ka-/ 'like'
to translate English 'as', and a whole range of makeshift phrases
to translate 'can', which is much commoner in English). Occasionally, he is so oppressed by the lack of a present of the verb
'to be' that he uses /maṭṭal/ 'represent'. And, above all, his
work is scattered with such familiar phrases as /waṣaḥīhan ʔan.../
'it is true that...' or /yajibu ʔan yudkara ʔan.../ 'it must be
pointed out that...'

Obviously, these features are most conspicuous in, for example,
translations of news releases which must be available for immediate broadcast. Their effect may be very slight in the works of
highly educated writers who are steeped in Arabic literature, so
that it is difficult to appraise their over-all impact. It is
generally true, however, that modern Arabic is becoming increasingly receptive to translation from Western languages, and this
is probably a necessary evolution.

3.144 <u>Formal efforts at language reform</u>[9]

There have been a number of efforts to coordinate the vocabulary
coinages of individuals and to control the modern developments
in Arabic. The Egyptian Linguistic Academy, founded in 1922, was
initially an independent organization of writers; it received
official sanction in 1932 and continues today. Syria has had a
Linguistic Academy since 1919, although it was somewhat eclipsed
during the French occupation. Other Arab countries have followed
suit with academies which encourage the publication of both classical and modern literature, 'pass' on suggested vocabulary coinages, propose new terms, and publish a journal to acquaint scholars with their activities. On the whole, the academies have not
been very successful in their normative efforts, and much of the
vocabulary they have sanctioned was never adopted. The development of separate academies in each country tended toward divi-
siveness, and in the thirties the academies began to try to
coordinate their efforts, starting with the official language of
treaties and the mails. Various professional groups have met to
try and deal with their special lexical problems: physicians

first in 1938, lawyers in 1944, engineers in 1946, and so on.
In 1956 the academies held a general conference in Damascus and
set up a coordinating committee to expedite their future work,
all very much in the spirit of Arab nationalism; a previous effort at coordination through the cultural committee of the Arab
League, established in 1946, had not been a success.

The academies have also been faced with very sweeping proposals for reform: 'simplifications' of Arabic grammar, the
adoption of colloquial Arabic for writing, orthographic reform.
The most drastic proposals, including latinization, have been
rejected, but the academies are much more sympathetic to attempts
at simplification. There have been a number of promising efforts
to simplify letter shapes so that they will vary less according
to their position in the word, thus substantially reducing the
cost of printing, and to provide for more information about the
vowels.

3.2 Speech (and writing) in Colloquial Arabic

As far back as our knowledge and conjecture can reach, a multitude of other dialects have existed alongside Classical Arabic.
The dialects have the obvious complementary characteristics to
ClA: they are considered less elevated, they are general to the
whole population (every Arab knows at least one as a first language), and they are regional and usually unwritten. They have
further characteristics: it is difficult to set their precise
boundaries, they are fluid over time, and they represent a more
advanced stage of developmental trends which can be seen in other
Semitic languages.

3.21 The origins of Colloquial Arabic

Because CoA is not normally written and the Arab grammarians
were only interested in the dialects to the extent that these
clarified odd constructions in ClA or as sources of error to be
rooted out of literary usage, the origins of the particular dialects of CoA now in existence are not clear. Three types of
hypothesis have been suggested: (a) that the modern dialects are

degenerate forms of Classical Arabic, reflecting a gradual deter-
ioration of usage which took place under the impact of the indigenous languages in the countries occupied by the Arab conquerors
(this is the traditional Arab explanation, with slight variations); (b) that the present dialects are lineal descendants of
pre-Islamic dialects spoken by the different tribes; (c) that
they are descendants of some form of intertribal speech in use
during the period of the conquests, containing a greater or
lesser admixture of ClA, and owe their variation to the indigenous influences[10].

The second hypothesis is eliminated by an examination of the
history of the conquests, since it is clear that in the original
invasions Arabs from all parts of the peninsula were thrown together, and the division of the garrison cities into tribal
quarters was a very fragile thing: even if we do not imagine the
immediate homogenization of these groups, particular tribes
emerged to dominate the situation in only a few areas. Furthermore, the dialects cannot be direct deteriorations of ClA since
ClA was never generally spoken and the dialects contain a few
features which seem to come directly from Semitic but do not
appear in ClA. The modern dialects outside of Arabia (that is,
in the areas conquered by the Arabs and colonized by them) seem
to be descended from a form of Arabic which was neither identical
to ClA nor homogeneous, but which included a whole range of dialect mixtures. Arab garrisons evidently developed a type of
speech which included more or less similar proportions of influence from the different tribal areas, depended on the tradition
of intertribal communication which had given rise to the poetic
koine, and was subjected to strong influences both from the
indigenous populations which rapidly adopted Arabic speech and
the Classical language itself. The homogeneity of this form of
speech was promoted by the movement of troops and individuals
from place to place, a fluidity which continued to some degree
right up to the decline of the ɛAbbāsid Empire, the Mongol and
Turkic invasions, and the nomadization of vast areas, which

drastically cut down on intercourse betweeen urban centers and
sedentary enclaves up to the modern period. The unity of this
range of dialects also stems from the fact that they were all
more innovative in the new linguistic environments, so that the
internal developmental trends of Arabic moved more swiftly in
all of these dialects than they had in nomadic Arabia or than
they seem to have moved in the existing nomadic dialects. In
contemporary discussions of Arabic dialectology, this range of
dialects is referred to as the Arabic koine, which must be care-
fully distinguished from the poetic koine. The effort is made
to deduce the features of this koine from the common features of
the dialects descended from it, which have since diverged considerably. Such a hypothesis is not refuted by the demonstration
that almost none of these features were completely common, since
a reconstructed koine is more a demonstration of a general con-
figuration than of a single uniform language believed to have
been spoken at a particular point in time.

The Arab invaders of the first Islamic centuries, who must have
spoken some form of this koine, merged with the local populations
by intermarriage and by assimilating the outsiders as clients to
their tribal groups, while these local populations (most of them
Christian) became converted to Islam. Local varieties of the
koine developed, and their speakers were almost completely seden-
tarized and became the ancestors of the city dwellers and villagers
of the modern Middle East, the speakers of sedentary dialects.
Members of later waves of migrations from the Arabian peninsula by
tribal groups, many of which still remain nomadic or semi-nomadic,
had not been involved in the formation of the koine but were somewhat more directly descended from the ancient dialects, and their
descendants speak dialects which may be roughly characterized
vis-à-vis the sedentary dialects as nomadic or Bedouin; the koine
hypothesis is essentially an effort to deal with the sedentary-
nomadic contrast, which is a striking one, although its dimensions
vary somewhat from place to place. In the contemporary Middle
East, it is no longer possible to say that all sedentary populations

speak sedentary dialects and nomadic populations nomadic dialects, since many nomads have settled and some settled groups have been uprooted. The Arabs are often romantic about their nomadic past, regarding corruption as an inevitable result of urban life and looking to the Bedouin as more noble and virile, and, especially, as speaking a purer form of Arabic, so that where large groups of speakers of nomadic dialects have mixed with sedentary populations, the dialect has tended to become nomadized, the Muslims adopting nomadic features more quickly than the Christian and Jewish minorities. In modern Baghdad, for instance, Muslims speak a nomadized dialect, while the minorities speak versions of a sedentary dialect which must originally have been spoken by the whole population. On the other hand, most of the nomadic invasions took place centuries ago, and there are regional characteristics cutting across sedentary-nomadic lines, so that it is possible to characterize all forms of Western Arabic vs. all forms of Eastern Arabic, or all forms of Mesopotamian Arabic vs. all other Eastern forms. Salient features of the dialects of the various large cities, which are of primary interest to the outsider, will be spelled out individually, but it is possible to state a series of developments which have taken place in all or nearly all forms of CoA, many of which can be recognized as part of the general developmental trend of Semitic, while others, occurring in the sedentary dialects, seem to point to a common origin in the hypothetical koine, especially when they are supplemented by a list of the contrasts between sedentary and nomadic dialects.

3.22 General trends of development in Colloquial Arabic

The most striking feature of CoA is that it has completely abandoned the system of nominal inflection for cases and verbal inflection for modes that existed in ClA by dropping all final short vowels. It is also generally more dependent on particles and word order than the classical language.

3.221 Phonology[11]

The points of the Classical system which were asymmetrical have been realigned in various ways. This realignment has affected

the interdentals and the ancient emphatic lateralized dental
fricative [ẓ^λ] which is transcribed in this handbook with its
most common modern pronunciation, /ḍ/, but appears in the dialects in a number of different ways. The role of the palatals
(/j/, /š/, /k/), and of the uvular /q/ has shifted. Emphasis
has been extended to /l/ and /r/ and affects other phonemes near
emphatics. Many short vowels (especially when unstressed, in
open syllables, and more frequently /i/ and /u/) have been lost
and long vowels shortened. Vowels have been affected by their
contexts so that the old triangular vowel system has broken down.
Diphthongs have been simplified to long vowels (/ay/ > /ē/ and
/aw/ > /ō/) which sometimes have corresponding shorts; this has
resulted in the development of a number of new syllable types
(containing clusters excluded by ClA) and has been accompanied
by the development of various sorts of stress.

By referring back to Sec. 1.2, it may be seen that these developments involve the loss of as many as four or five consonant
phonemes (1.21) balanced by increased complexity of vowels (1.22)
and syllable structure (1.23), while (1.24) the contrast of pause
vs. context forms has been dropped, and stress has become more
important (but variable from place to place).

3.222 Morphology

The loss of final short vowels (iɛrāb), sometimes referred to as
the generalization of pause forms, accompanied by the generalization of the genitive-accusative forms of duals and sound masculine
plurals, has been part of a general reduction in inflectional
categories. Similarly, the dual has retrogressed in all of the
dialects: it survives to some degree in the noun, but has disappeared from all pronominal or verbal forms, and dual nouns are
treated, for the purpose of agreement, like animate plurals. The
morphological processes described in 1.311 are all abandoned except determination by the definite article; this is complemented
by an increase in syntactic complexity, including the frequent
adoption of some form of indefinite article; residues of the
pause-context contrast appear in the special forms which some

nouns, especially feminine singulars and sound masculine plurals, take when they are in construct. (Residues of the accusative indefinite used adverbially are discussed under syntax.) The remaining categories of noun morphology and the system of nominal derivation are relatively stable, except that the number of noun types may be greatly reduced by the loss of short vowels (although aberrant types are often accepted), e.g. the loss of all unstressed short vowels in open syllables means that such contrasting sets as CaCāC—CiCāC—CuCāC or CaCūC—CuCūC are lost, and of course the functional specializations originally associated with these patterns tend to be blurred.

The Arabic number system (1.33) is everywhere radically simplified by the loss of iɛrāb; this simplification has been carried even further, however, in dialects outside of Arabia, and has striking common features in most of the Eastern sedentary dialects and in many Western ones: the anomalous handling of gender in ClA has been repatterned so that all counting is done with the old feminine forms (with no noun following) while enumerating is done with the old masculine forms, regardless of the gender of the following noun: Syr. /xamse/ 'five (the name of the number)' but /xams wlād/ 'five boys' and /xams banāt/ 'five girls' vs. ClA /xamsatu ʔawlād/ and /xamsu banāt/; residues of the ClA gender inversion remain in a number of special plurals used in enumerating which have an extraneous /t/: /xams tušhur/ 'five months' /xams tiyyām/ 'five days' vs. ClA /xamsatu ʔašhur/, /xamsatu ʔayyām/; furthermore, the '-teens' have been compounded into single words based on the ClA masculine: /xamsṭaɛš/ 'fifteen', with an emphatic /ṭ/, ClA /xamsata ɛašara/.

Verbal inflection (1.41) is simplified by the loss of all dual forms, while mode has ceased to be expressed by inflectional endings. However, almost all the dialects have introduced a prefix for the indicative (Syr. /birūḥ/ 'he goes' for the indicative, vs. /yrūḥ/ after a verb or particle expressing intention) and a number of ways of indicating tense more precisely, sometimes with a three-way system for past-present-future. The number of types of 'weak' verbs (1.413-15) are reduced in all dialects, but it is striking that these reductions, that is, the solution of a problem faced by all the dialects, were reached in a similar manner in most sedentary dialects (descended from the koine): C_3=/w/ verbs are treated exactly like the commoner C_3=/y/ (this is true of all derived verbs in ClA), while C_2=C_3 verbs are treated in the perfect like Form II final weak verbs: Syr. /maddēt/ 'I continued' (Form I) and /ṣallēt/ 'I prayed' (Form II) vs. ClA /madadtu/, /ṣallaytu/. In the area of verb derivation, the distinctions of the primary verb vowel patterns tend to be blurred, but the major derived forms survive, although sometimes only one or two examples of some forms can be discovered. The internal passive (1.4221) has disappeared except in Saudi, again probably in relation to the decay of the short vowel system. The system of particles is expanded, and has an amplified importance, while the number of pronouns is reduced, parallel to the reduction in verb forms. In place of the ClA relative pronoun system, the dialects generally have only a single form.

3.223 Syntax

The major changes are directly related to morphological changes, as the language becomes increasingly synthetic and word order bears a heavier burden. CoA may have a more complex system of parts of speech than ClA as some dialects have developed an autonomous category of adverbs, many of them borrowed from ClA (Syr. /jiddan/ 'very', using the indefinite accusative ending). Phrase types, especially verbal phrases, are multiplied, and in many areas the typical sentence order is like that of English, where the subject precedes the verb.

3.224 Lexicon

The various dialects are always more hospitable to loanwords than ClA, but the primary source language varies from place to place (see 3.42). A conspicuous difference is that many varieties of CoA contain Turkish loanwords, which are extremely rare in ClA. Almost everywhere the doubly weak verb /raʔā/ 'see' has been replaced by /šāf yšūf/; the Classical /jāʔa bi-/ 'come with, bring' has been reshaped into /jāb yjīb/ 'bring'; and new forms have been adopted for 'what' (ClA /mā/, which had several different functions, now replaced by /ʔēš/, /šū/, etc.).

3.225 Summary

The loss of inflectional categories is the most obvious aspect of the ClA-CoA contrast, but equally important is the decline in importance of the almost algebraic root system of Classical due to (a) the increase in particles, which play a more important role as they carry the functions which were originally carried by inflection; (b) the loss or merger of derivational patterns so that word forms seem increasingly arbitrary; (c) the further separation of the semivowels from the consonantal system via the decay of diphthongs, the simplification of 'weak' verb inflection, and the shortening of final long vowels; (d) a general shift in the phonological shape of the word with a rise in assimilation and allophonic variation.

3.23 Variation in Colloquial Arabic

CoA varies in many different dimensions and has no single norm. In order to cover this wide range with some degree of efficiency, no single dialect will be fully described in the following sections, but certain fundamental features of groups of dialects may be inferred by interpreting the general trends of CoA in terms of (1) the nomadic-sedentary contrast and (2) the various geographical regions, with some specifics of the major prestige dialects.

3.231 Contrasts between sedentary and nomadic dialects

Just as the loss of case endings is the obvious point of contrast between ClA and CoA, so it is possible to point to a single obvious distinction between sedentary and nomadic dialects: all sedentary dialects have voiceless versions of the Classical phoneme noted as /q/: [ʔ] in most cities of Syria and Egypt, [k] for some rural Palestinian dialects, [q] in Iraq and most of North Africa; whereas nomadic dialects have a voiced consonant, typically [g]. This is the only feature that occurs in all nomadic-sedentary contrasts outside of Arabia.

Most sedentary dialects have lost the interdentals, turning them into stops, so that nomadic [t̲], [d̲], and [ḏ] (the last a reflex of both ClA /ẓ/ and /ḏ/) are generally [t], [d], and [ḍ] in sedentary dialects. However, there are sedentary groups using the interdentals scattered in the Fertile Crescent, and they survive in the major sedentary dialect of Tunisia.

Sedentary dialects have lost gender distinctions in the plural of verbs and pronouns. Combined with the elimination of dual forms this leads to a great simplification, since, of the thirty-six forms shown on the chart of verbal inflections in 1.411 (Table 3), at least ten are eliminated, and a similar simplification affects the pronouns.

Sedentary dialects have adopted various particles meaning 'belonging to, associated with', which are used in addition to the construct; Mor. /sseyyāra māl lmūdīr/ 'the director's car'; Syr. /ssayyāra tabaɛī/ 'my car', where ClA would have /sayyāratu lmudīr/ and /sayyāratī/ only; both /tabaɛ/ and /māl/ are used with following nouns or pronouns. Another relatively consistent sedentary supplement to the system of particles is a particle used with a verb to express continuous action: Eg. /ɛammāl/, /ɛamm/, Mor. /kā/.

3.232 Eastern and Western Colloquial Arabic

Whereas the nomadic-sedentary contrast covers the whole of the Arabic-speaking world, preserving the record of two ways of life which have been important throughout the area and of two major stages of Arabic-speaking migration following after the other Semitic migrations of previous centuries, the present-day Arab world is divided into a number of different areas by regional dialect characteristics. These regional variations are very old and were first described in the middle of the tenth century by the geographer al-Muqaddasī. They correspond only roughly to modern political boundaries, so that 'Moroccan Arabic' and 'Syrian Arabic', for example, do not refer to forms of Arabic spoken throughout these countries and contrasting with the forms spoken in neighboring countries, but to the dialect norms of

major cities which tend to be regarded as prestige dialects in
the areas administered from those cities, even though the surrounding countryside is a patchwork of different dialect forms,
some of them nomadic and some of them very close to the dialect
of the capital of the neighboring country.

The regional dialects form two main clusters: Eastern Arabic,
which is spoken throughout the Fertile Crescent; by Syrian and
Lebanese emigré communities in the Americas; in all the Arabic-
speaking regions of Asia (including enclaves of an Iraqi-like
nomadic dialect in the USSR); in Egypt and the Sudan (where
Arabic is side by side with various African languages), and in
all areas of East Africa which have been partially Arabized by
influences down through the Sudan or across the Red Sea and down
the coast (the Arabic of Somalia is Yemenite, that of Zanzibar
is like Oman); and Western Arabic, the dialect spoken in the
region referred to as the Maghreb, namely Morocco, Algeria,
Tunisia, and most of Libya, filtering down into the French
territories of sub-Saharan West Africa. Eastern and Western
Arabic meet and mix around Lake Chad. Again, this division can
be attached to a single contrasting feature: in the Eastern dialects, the basic ClA pattern of prefixes for the imperfect is
retained (see 1.411), simplified only by the elimination of
duals and feminine plurals: in the second and third persons,
the singular-plural contrast depends on the suffix (third person
masc. sing. /y-/ vs. third person masc. pl. /y--u/; second person masc. sing. /t-/ vs. second person masc. pl. /t--u/); while
in the first person there is no plural suffix and the contrast
is expressed by the prefix (first person sing. /ʔ(a)-/ vs.
first person pl. /n-/). In the Western dialects, the /-u/ suffix has been generalized to all persons of the plural, and the
'we' prefix to all first persons, so that the first person singular has the form /n-/ and the plural has /n--u/: Mor. /nsedd/
'I close' vs. /nseddu/ 'we close'.

There are a number of other, less striking, contrasts:
Western dialects tend to lose /ʔ/, which is much more

generally retained in the East; as a result, they have a greater
variety of vowel clusters and diphthongs. In all the Western
dialects, vocalic changes have been more drastic than in the
East: commonly, all short vowels in open syllables have been
lost, so that only long syllables (Cv̄ or CvC) survive (e.g.
ClA /šarib/ > Mor. /šreb/). The loss of final short vowels resulted everywhere in final clusters: in the East (except Egypt),
where these clusters were difficult to pronounce, vowels were
inserted: Ir. /ḥarb/ 'war' but /ṣubuḥ/ 'morning', ClA /ṣubḥ/;
in the West, wherever this insertion of a vowel after the second
consonant took place, it left the first vowel in an open syllable, so that it was dropped: ClA /qabr/ > */qabar/ > Mor.
/qbar/ 'tomb'. Furthermore, whereas most Eastern dialects tend
to retain /a/ even in positions where /i/ and /u/ are lost,
Western does not.

In addition to the special first person forms of the imperfect, Western Arabic has made a number of derivational innova-
tions with, in some cases, new derived verbs rounding out the
ClA pattern and a form with prefixed /t-/~/tt-/ functioning like
ClA Form VII: Mor. /tekteb/ (cf. ClA /nkatab/, 'be written').
Because of the slighter revision of the vowel system, Eastern
dialects tend, in part, to retain the different vowel patterns
of primary verbs: Syr. /btuktub/ 'you write', /btišrab/ 'you
drink'.

There are also very striking differences in vocabulary, with
items that are used throughout the whole of one dialect area
being completely unknown in another.

3.233 Iraqi Arabic[12]

The prestige dialect of Iraq, which is the one most likely to be
studied by outsiders, is the dialect of the Muslim population of
Baghdad. This is one of several dialect varieties spoken in
Iraq, some of which extend quite a distance outside of the political boundaries of the country, and which belong to a type of
Arabic referred to as Mesopotamian, or 'Eastern Arabic'. This
dialect is spoken in a broad band running from Kuwait on the

Persian Gulf through all of Iraq and up into Arabic-speaking areas in southeastern Turkey, including eastern Syria, around Palmyra and as far west as the area of Aleppo; related forms are spoken in southern Iran and in the Soviet Union. Only in Iraq, however, is it the prestige dialect of large metropolitan and administrative centers. In general, the area is characterized by (a) the phonemes /p/, /č/, and /j/ =[dž], which have varying etymologies: all are reinforced by the many Turkish and Iranian loanwords in the dialect, and /k/ appears with varying consistency as the reflex of ClA /k/; (b) the preservation of ClA interdentals and diphthongs (side by side with /ē/ and /ō/) over most of the area; (c) various reflexes of ClA /q/ (but never /ʔ/); (d) the preservation of /-n/ after the long vowel suffixes of the imperfect: /yisuknūn/ 'they live', /trīdīn/ 'you (fem.) wish' vs. ClA /yaskunūn/ and /turīdīn/; (e) a characteristic construction suffixing the appropriate pronoun to a transitive verb and then prefixing /l-/ to the noun object: /ma aḥibba lhāda/ 'I don't like this one', where /aḥibb/ is 'I like' and /-a/ is the dialectal form of the third person singular pronoun suffix (ClA /-hu/); (f) characteristic lexical items, such as /fadd/ 'a, an (indefinite article)', and /māl/ 'belonging to' (as an alternative to the construct); and throughout the lexicon. Iraq is often called 'the land of /aku/ and /māku/', which mean 'there is' and 'there is not' in this region. Other words special to this dialect area are /hassa/ 'now', /mēz/ 'table', and /bazzūna/ 'cat', as well as a very large number of Turkish and Persian loans.[13]

The Muslim dialect of Baghdad, while it clearly belongs to the Iraqi regional type, is a nomadic dialect, with a voiced reflex of ClA /q/: /gelet/ 'I said' (cf. ClA /qultu/). Sedentary dialects, still spoken in the historic cities of the north of Iraq, Mosul, Tikrīt, etc., and in the sedentary regions of eastern Syria, have /qeltu/ 'I said'. These dialects dominated the area until the drastic breakdown of urban control, with accompanying anarchy and nomadic invasions, after the sack of Baghdad

in 1258; this trend continued for five centuries, and when the
tide turned in the eighteenth century and city life began to
develop again, the old sedentary Muslim populations were so
heavily infiltrated by speakers of nomadic dialects that their
dialects were Bedouinized. In Upper Iraq, the devastation was
slighter and /qeltu/ dialects are still used by settled populations; in Lower Iraq, /qeltu/ dialects only survived among
Jewish and Christian minority groups (see 3.237). In general,
the phonology of the Baghdad dialect is more like ClA, whereas
the old sedentary dialects have /č/ for ClA /k/ in many environments, /ġ/ for ClA /r/, and more imāla (inclination of /a/ toward
/i/): Baghdad /jāmeɛ/ 'mosque' vs. Mosul /jēmeɛ/.

3.234 Syrian Arabic

Syrian Arabic is a construct based on the remarkably similar dialects spoken by the population of several important cities of
eastern Syria, Palestine, and Lebanon, especially Damascus,
Jerusalem, and Beirut; it is sometimes referred to as Eastern
Mediterranean Arabic and is the prestige dialect of Syria,
Lebanon, and Jordan. Urban settlement has been more stable in
this area, and although nomadic dialects are used in a few places
in the country and in the desert areas, agricultural towns and
villages speak dialects going back to the koine. These city
dialects have /ʔ/ for ClA /q/, /k/ for ClA /k/, /j/=[ž], and have
completely lost the interdentals, which have become /t/, /d/, and
/ḍ/. Long /ā/ has been stable and short /a/ has been relatively
stable everywhere except in the feminine ending, which has imāla:
/madrase/ 'school', ClA /madrasah/. The loss of diphthongs,
which have only survived as doubled semivowels, and otherwise
have been simplified to /ē/ and /ō/, e.g. /bēt/ 'house', ClA
/bayt/, occurred in this area except in a large part of Lebanon.
Corresponding to the specific lexical items cited for Iraq,
Syrian Arabic has: /fī/, /mā fī/, 'there is', 'there is not';
/wāḥid/ 'a, an' for the indefinite article; /tabaɛ/ (~/šīt/ in
Damascus, /šēt/ in Jerusalem) 'belonging to'; /halla/ or /hallaʔ/
'now'; /ṭāwla/ 'table'; and /bisse/ 'cat'; the last two forms are

derived from ClA. Syrian Arabic contrasts with ClA and with most other dialects, which would use an auxiliary verb, in using /bidd-/ with suffixed pronoun to express a wish: /biddī ʔarūḥ/ 'I want to go'.

3.235 Egyptian Arabic

Egyptian Arabic is more similar to Syrian Arabic than the latter is to Iraqi, for it is also an Oriental sedentary dialect—that is, both fall on the same side of the East-West contrast and the sedentary-nomadic contrast. In Upper (southern) Egypt, Bedouinized dialects are spoken which contrast quite radically with the prestige dialect of Cairo, but the Cairene influence is spreading.

Cairene Arabic contrasts with Syrian Arabic in that it has ClA /j/=[g]: Egypt is the 'land of the gīm', and although ClA /q/ has become /ʔ/ in all true colloquial words, there are more Classical loans in common usage, so that /q/ is quite frequent. Egyptian Arabic also has a stress pattern which contrasts with Syrian: Eg. /madrása/ 'school' vs. Syr. /mádrase/. In general, Syrian accent falls on the v̄C or vCC nearest the end of the word or, if no such sequence appears, on the first syllable. In Egyptian, the same syllable types would draw the accent to the final syllable; otherwise it generally falls on the penultimate syllable.

For the lexical items already mentioned: /wāḥid/ 'a, an', /fī/, /ma fīš/ 'there is', 'there is not' (š̌ appears for negation in many varieties of Oriental Arabic); /bitāɛ/~/mitāɛ/ 'belonging to'; /dilwaʔti/ 'now' (Egyptian Arabic is the only major city dialect that has lost the /hā-/ of the ClA demonstratives; cf. ClA /hādā lwaqt/ 'this time'); /ṭaṛabēza/ 'table'; /ʔuṭṭa/ 'cat'. Egyptians tend to be highly amused by the /xāṭrak/ with which Syrians begin the series of polite formulae that accompany departure, since this is never used in Egypt.

3.236 North African Arabic

Dialect boundaries in the Maghreb do not correspond particularly well with political boundaries and are better explained with

reference to the linguistic layers that have affected the whole
North African littoral. Unlike the countries that have been discussed so far, the language which was in use before the Arab invasions is still in extensive use: there are four million speakers
of Berber in Morocco, two and a half million in Algeria, and much
smaller numbers in Tunisia and Libya; Berber speakers are concen-
trated in the back country, and their influence shows primarily
in rural dialects of Arabic such as in the mountainous areas of
Morocco: odd variants of the dentals, [ts] or [t^y], and a great
deal of loan vocabulary. North Africa was conquered by the Arabs
in the seventh and eighth centuries, but only some 150,000 troops
settled there, while the greater number pressed on to Spain.
North Africa was thinly settled and the Arabs stayed in cities
like Tangier along the coast, although some of these settlements
were later pushed to rural areas such as Jbala. Later, when
Spain was reconquered by the Christians, Muslims left in wave
after wave of exiles, establishing new dynasties and founding
some new cities, like Fez, further in the interior. Old Arabic
dialects in North Africa, then, show various degrees of Berber
influence and reflect two strands of dialect descended from the
koine, one of which developed in Spain, while the other developed
in various pockets of settlement among those who did not move on
to Spain. Nomadic Arabic swept across North Africa in the
eleventh and twelfth centuries, brought by Beni Hilal tribesmen
from southern Arabia, estimated at about 200,000, and other
tribal groups have followed. Some cities, e.g. Gabès in Tunisia,
Marrakesh in Morocco, or Oran and towns near Algiers in Algeria,
speak Bedouin dialects, often with non-Muslim minorities still
preserving the old urban dialects descended from the koine, but
the majority of urban centers retain urban dialects, many rural
areas show strong Bedouin influences, and the whole nomadic
Arabic-speaking population speaks nomadic type Arabic. The nomadic and urban speakers must strain to understand each other.

There is of course considerable variation from city to city.
The urban dialects of Libya and some parts of Tunisia reduce ClA

/j/ to [z] in some contexts: /zūz/ 'pair', ClA /zawj/. Tunisian
dialects seem to have considerable short vowel variation, and
have omitted the very common development of an indefinite article
(developed from variations on /wāḥid/ elsewhere) and a substitute for iḏāfa. Moroccan forms for the other lexical items that
have been mentioned are /kāy^en/, /ma kāy^enš/ 'there is', 'there
is not'; /d-/∼/dyāl/∼/mtāɛ/ 'of, belonging to'; /mīda/ 'table';
and /qeṭṭa/ 'cat'.

The dialect spoken on the island of Malta, which is now completely Christian and was for some time a British Protectorate
after a long period of Italian rule, seems to be a variant of
North African urban Arabic. Maltese has suffered such a flood
of Italian loanwords and is so drastically distorted in its
phonology and syntax that it was once considered no more than a
very strange and deviant dialect of Italian. However, the morphology is quite clearly descended from koine Arabic. Maltese
is of some interest because it is a form of Colloquial Arabic
which has been completely separated from any ClA influence; it
is written in a special latin letter alphabet designed for it,
and is beginning to produce some literature. Even in the Soviet
Union, where Arabic speakers now have a Cyrillic orthography for
their dialects and are encouraged to use it, some Classical influence is maintained.

3.237 Communal dialects

In the history of some cities of the Arab world, dialectal shifts
have taken place which have left religious minorities speaking
special dialects. These are at present usually Christian minorities since in most places the Jewish colonies that were equally
affected by this split are either in Israel, where their special
Arabic dialects may be expected to die out, or they are doing
their best to be inconspicuous, which may mean adopting the
majority dialect. In most places the separate community life of
the minority has fostered slight dialect differences, especially
in vocabulary (the Jews have tended to use a good deal of Hebrew
vocabulary), and the greater tendency of Christians to be educated

in European-sponsored schools may foster special loanwords, so
that is is often possible to recognize members of minority communities by their speech, although many Christians or Jews have
learned to control the majority dialect and may boast that they
can 'speak like a Muslim' in the market. In most places the
minority populations are urban and really drastic differences
only develop as a result of major shifts in population such as
the Bedouinization of Lower Iraq and some North African cities.

3.24 Influences of Classical Arabic and interdialectal influences

There are a number of points at which Classical forms regularly
invade CoA. Throughout the Arab world, there are formulae which
may be pronounced in partial conformity with the phonology of
the region but preserve ClA case endings. Many of these are
formal phrases of etiquette, since Arabic is particularly rich
in sequences of polite remarks each having an appropriate response, sometimes forming a whole chain: appropriate wishes for
each time of day; phrases to be used in greeting someone who is
eating, someone who has just had a drink, someone who has bathed
or had a haircut; phrases used to ward off misfortune when ad-
miring something or inquiring about someone's family; extravagant
offers of hospitality. Others are curses or exclamations. CoA
also borrows a great deal of vocabulary from ClA. Educated
speakers draw on the education they have received in a Classical
context whenever they are discussing technical or academic subjects, and many such words enter the general vocabulary, sometimes via the radio or cinema. Much religious vocabulary is
borrowed from ClA: in Jerusalem, for instance, where ClA /q/
normally becomes /ʔ/, /q/ is still pronounced in the word
/qurʔān/, and Cairo Arabic has a considerable number of ClA
loanwords preserving /q/. The same Classical word may have two
cognates in CoA, one of which has followed the normal evolution
of the dialect while the other has been borrowed. In areas
where the interdentals are reduced to dentals by the dialect
they are pronounced as sibilants in Classical loanwords, so that
ClA /ḥadīt̠/ 'event, saying' yields both /ḥadīt/ 'event' and

/ḥadīs/ 'saying attributed to Muḥammad'. Proverbs, including religious maxims, are often quoted in ClA, and a number of recognizable ClA proverbs are part of the inventory of illiterate speakers.

Influences between the dialects tend to occur in relation to the prestige dialect of an area, so that there is a tendency for the dialect of the capital to spread into the surrounding countryside, since it is generally necessary to learn it in order to participate in the national life, and for non-Muslims to imitate the Muslim dialect. This tends toward the enhancement of the dialect of the capital and an increasing tendency for dialect boundaries to correspond to national boundaries. Egyptian Arabic, through radio broadcasting and films, is the only sedentary dialect which is presently influencing other regions. There is also a continuing tendency among young people in poor rural areas to imitate nearby Bedouin groups.

Because of the difficulties of diglossia, there has been a good deal of talk about the possibilities of developing a 'middle language', a form of Arabic which would lack the complexities of ClA and yet be understandable throughout the Arab world and maintain contact with the Classical tradition. At present, intellectuals from different Arab countries have several alternatives in speaking to each other: (a) they may speak or try to speak ClA, which imposes a great deal of strain and formalism; (b) they may speak French or English; or (c) they may try to use their own forms of CoA for a maximum of communication. Their education gives them the resources for this last which might be impossible to villagers from the same regions. The principal means of educated interdialectal conversation have been described as 'classicizing' and 'leveling'.[14] 'Classicizing' may be very superficial, using items which are associated with educated speech even within a dialect region but do not add much to the communicative value: introducing clauses with /ʔan/ without changing their basic syntax, restoring some short vowels and /q/, and using /fa-/ frequently although all the dialects have /wa-/. Classical

vocabulary is freely borrowed, as it is in all educated (and
pretentious) speech. 'Leveling' involves underplaying those
features of the speaker's dialect which are known to be aberrant
or are considered so in the Arabs' mythology about their dialects
and selecting among alternatives those features which are most
like ClA. Often leveling takes place more in relation to the
prestige dialect of the speaker's own region than to the dialect
of his companion. Leveling may take place without particular
reference to ClA, as in the kind of 'normalized Bedouin' which
was spoken by nomadic recruits from different tribal areas while
they did army service during the French occupation of Syria,[15]
and suggests one process which must have been operative in the
formation of the koine.

3.25   The use of Colloquial Arabic

Colloquial Arabic is used in all of the contexts which do not
demand the use of Classical. At first glance, these may seem
quite limited, but in fact they make up the major part of life:
CoA is the only language of a great many inhabitants of Arab
countries; it is used in almost all conversation with servants
or workmen, in the street or in the market, and in most informal
conversation with colleagues even in academic or political cir-
cles. Most important, CoA is the only language which is ever
used in the home, and Arabs who advocate the complete adoption
of ClA find the idea of speaking it to their own children ludi-
crous. On the other hand, because CoA is felt to lack eloquence
and structure, children receive little or no formal training in
manipulating it. Between a quarter and a half of the total time
in elementary school is spent on gaining a bare mastery of Classical Arabic. Modern methods have brought some concern for
developing the child's ability to order and express his thought,
side by side with the traditional training in rhetoric which
accompanies reading and writing, grammar and memorization, but
almost none of this time is spent on developing language skills
in the actual spoken language. CoA is the mother tongue of the
Arab and remains throughout his life the primary medium of

interpersonal relationships, especially intimate ones, but it is never developed as the medium for abstract thought. Many Arabs use both CoA and ClA, but their knowledge of each is specialized and their fluency is always situational; the use of the wrong variety in a particular situation is felt as extremely inappropriate. However, many Arabs do feel that their local dialect is closer to the Classical than any other.

CoA invades the specifically Classical spheres of broadcasting, literature, and publishing in a number of circumscribed ways: it may be used for dialogue in radio plays or movies and often in print, especially in the captions of cartoons or in humorous or anecdotal material. Writing Colloquial in the Arabic alphabet is governed by fluctuating conventions, but the normalization implied by the omission of the vowels and so on, makes written CoA appear to deviate less from ClA than it actually does. In conservative transcriptions the article is usually written according to the ClA convention (always with the letter for /l/ since the assimilation to following apicals is automatic), and the feminine ending is indicated by the letter for /h/. Because of the differences in phonology, Western scholars now almost always use a transcription based on latin letter forms for writing CoA, which may or may not reflect a full phonological analysis of the dialect.

There are also several branches of Arabic literature where CoA is the norm, although historically these have been outside of the main stream. First of all, the composition and recitation of poetry has remained a part of nomadic life, usually in slightly different dialectal form from that used in actual speech and closely surrounded by convention. Rural sedentary areas have also developed rich folklore traditions, with a slightly wider range, including songs and some semi-dramatic forms. Most of what we possess of this folk literature has been collected by Western orientalists or linguists, but there has been some interest in this tradition on the part of Arabs, especially where, as in Lebanon, the Pan-Arab identification is low and there is an interest in regional folk traditions and collections of songs and proverbs have been made. Some of this interest has gone even further and combined with the unease many Arab writers feel about writing dialogue or describing domestic or village life in ClA, so that a number of writers have experimented with novels or plays in CoA, vacillating between ClA and CoA, or even issuing their work in two versions, one in CoA and one in ClA, for wider circulation in other dialect areas. There were two movements toward a written literary production in CoA in the medieval period: a vulgar poetry of the cities of Iraq and songs, especially of the type called zajal, in Andalusia and North Africa.

Not surprisingly, the influence of the ClA norm has been weaker among non-Muslim minorities. CoA appears in texts written by Christians and Jews living under Arab Islamic rule as early as the ninth century; these were primarily non-literary prose texts which reflect efforts to approximate ClA by populations which had not fully mastered it and were clearly speaking forms of Arabic very like the present-day urban dialects. Since they are all in the Arabic alphabet and attempt to follow ClA norms, the features of this 'Middle Arabic'[16] have to be deduced from errors and from hypercorrect forms, but it seems clear that Middle Arabic had already lost the final short vowels, with the stabilization of word order this implies, reduced its inflectional categories (duals only in the noun, a single relative pronoun), etc. Most of the recognizable features of Middle Arabic are those which are attributed to the koine and characterize modern and sedentary dialects in general, although there is some local variation and a slight variation between Christian and Jewish texts. Many leaders in the modernization of ClA were Christians who stressed their right to a full Arab identity through the language, but in some areas, especially Lebanon, North Africa, and the Yemen, the ClA norm has been weaker for Christians and Jews, who have been more apt to write CoA forms.

3.3 Speech and writing in other languages

In the Arab world, a number of other languages are used. These
fall into two categories: indigenous minority languages which,
for their speakers, precede the knowledge of Arabic necessary
for full participation in the national life; and European languages which are learned as second (or third) languages by both
speakers of Arabic and speakers of the minority languages, and
open up the possibilities of education and communication in terms
of European culture. The most important indigenous languages are:

(1) Berber (see 3.236), a distant relative of Arabic which was
the old language of North Africa and is still spoken by a
third of the population of Morocco and a fifth of that of
Algeria. Berber is not used administratively and is actively
discouraged by the Arab governments. In most areas it is
purely a spoken language, but the roman alphabet has been
adopted in Kabylia and there is a certain amount of popular
literature.

(2) Kurdish, the Indo-European language of the Kurds which is
closely related to Persian. The Kurds live in a number of
different countries, including Iran, Turkey, and the Soviet
Union, but the largest group in any Arabic-speaking country
is in northern Iraq. Kurdish tribesmen have been in rebellion against the central government for a number of years,
and one of the issues has been the possibility of using
their language in administration and in higher education.
There is some publishing in Kurdish, using the Arabic alphabet, in Iraq. A modified Cyrillic alphabet is used by
Kurdish speakers in the Soviet Union and large quantities
of written and broadcast revolutionary propaganda in Kurdish
originate there, but the body of literature in Kurdish is
quite small.

(3) Armenian, another Indo-European language with no close relatives within that superfamily. Small groups of Armenian
merchants established colonies in most of the large cities
of the Middle East during the period of the Ottoman Empire,

and there is a very old colony in Jerusalem, but the large
colonies that can now be found in Syria, especially in
Aleppo, and around Beirut are mainly composed of survivors
of the Turkish deportations during World War I when hundreds
of thousands of Armenians were driven into the Syrian desert.
Armenian has two principal dialects, one (Eastern Armenian)
spoken by Armenians living in and around the present Soviet
Socialist Republic of Armenia and in Iran, and the other
(Western Armenian) spoken by Armenians descended from the
subjects of the medieval Armenian kingdom of Cilicia which
was founded by a group of Armenians that migrated to Asia
Minor, outside of traditional Armenian territory. The Turkish
oppressions destroyed the population concentrations in present-
day Turkish territory, but there is a contemporary cultural
center of western Armenians in the Arab world. Armenians run
schools (which are now required to dedicate a great deal of
time to Arabic), publish newspapers, and carry on a considerable literary production; large quarters of some cities,
especially Beirut and Jerusalem, are Armenian. Classical
Armenian is the liturgical language of the Armenian Apostolic
Church, and there are also Protestant and Eastern-rite Catholic groups using the language and maintaining important
establishments. Unlike the Berbers and the Kurds, the Armenians are richer and better educated than the Muslims
around them; their participation in government is limited
in some places, but they produce many merchants and professional men, including many of the doctors.

(4) A number of other languages of less importance are still
used: South Arabic (see 2.1) survives in a small region
along the southern coast of Arabia. Syriac-Aramaic (see 2.1)
includes Classical Syriac, which is used liturgically by a
number of Eastern churches; Neo-Syriac, a language spoken by
a number of non-Muslims in Iran and Iraq; and Aramaic, in a
few pockets in the Syrian dialect area. Coptic is used
liturgically in Egypt but has not been spoken for several

centuries, and there are a few speakers of Turkmen or of the
Turkish of Turkey, and of Circassian, a Caucasian language.

For all of these indigenous languages, although there may be
large numbers of speakers who know no Arabic, the majority of
these are women, while the men have learned at least a minimal
amount of Arabic for dealing with the government. The Armenians
will probably carry on an autonomous cultural life for a long
time to come, but there is no proposal to set up separate administrative districts for them. There might be a great practical
gain in extending the use of Berber and Kurdish, but the Arab
governments are uniformly opposed to this.

There is also widespread knowledge of European languages in
the Arab world, depending on the occupying countries during the
period after World War I: in most of North Africa and in Syria
and Lebanon, French is the prevailing European language; both
French and English have been important in Egypt; and in the Sudan,
Arabia, Jordan, and Iraq, English has a greater influence. Italian is the commonest second language of Libya but the influence of
English is increasing, and Spanish is known in Spanish Morocco.
The knowledge of a major European language is everywhere an advantage, but in North Africa this has been carried to a point
where it threatens the Arab identity of the country.[17] During the
French occupation, the number of European settlers exceeded the
number of Arabs who originally Arabized North Africa, and the
French made every effort to discourage Arabic culture. One-third
of the population of Morocco and a half of the populations of
Algeria and Tunisia speak French, and more people are literate
in French than in Arabic. French is extensively used in the
schools and in government and although the present policy is in
favor of Arabization, the North African leaders want to retain
French and the access to French culture and lack sufficient
trained Arabs to maintain an effective Arabization program.

In the French-influenced countries of the Levant this has not
occurred because there was never an extensive colonization and
the term of French control was shorter. Whereas in North Africa

no higher education or participation in government is possible for a monolingual, it is now fully possible to study such fields as law or medicine in Arabic at Arab universities in Cairo, Alexandria, Baghdad, and Damascus; literacy in Arabic is higher, and, except for minority groups like the Armenians and some Christian Arabs, literacy in Arabic normally precedes literacy in French. Many Christians maintain their knowledge of French as part of their identification with Europe, and an ability to speak French is a mark of the educated bourgeoisie, but it is not the only way of gaining access to a general education. English has penetrated even less, so that nowhere in the region where Eastern dialects are spoken is there any question but that Arabic is the primary medium of literacy for the Muslim population.

NOTES

1. Chaim Rabin, Ancient West Arabian (London, 1951).

2. The outstanding example of this is the melhūn, a classicized and Bedouinized dialect used in North Africa for poetry; cf. G. Colin, 'L'arabe', in Initiation au Maroc, ed. Louis Brunot (Paris, 1945), p. 225. For similar examples, cf. R. Blachère, Histoire de la littérature arabe (Paris, 1952), p. 80.

3. Johann Fück, ʿArabīya, Recherches sur l'histoire de la langue et du style arabe, tr. Claude Denizeau (Paris, 1955).

4. Charles A. Ferguson, 'Diglossia', Word 15.325-40 (1959).

5. UNESCO, World Illiteracy at Mid-Century (Paris, 1957).

6. Most of the examples in this section are taken from Vincent Monteil, L'arabe moderne (Paris, 1960).

7. Richard S. Harrell, Contributions to Arabic Linguistics, ed. Charles A. Ferguson (Cambridge, Mass., 1960) p. 9, 15.

8. Similar problems and processes have been described for modern Hebrew by Haim Blanc in 'Hebrew in Israel: Trends and Problems', Middle East Journal 11.397-409 (1957).

9. Anwar Chejne, 'The Role of Arabic in Present-Day Arab Society', The Islamic Literature 10:4.15-54 (1958).

10. Charles A. Ferguson, 'The Arabic Koine', Language 35.616-30 (1959); and David Cohen, 'Koinè, langues communes et dialectes arabes', Arabica 9.119-44 (1962).

11. Jean Cantineau, Cours de phonétique arabe (Paris, 1960).

12. Haim Blanc, Communal Dialects in Baghdad (Cambridge, Mass., 1964).

13. Charles A. Ferguson and Majed Sa'īd, 'Lexical Variants in Arabic Dialects' [1958, mimeo.] has been used for almost all the lexical examples.

14. Haim Blanc, 'Stylistic Variations in Spoken Arabic: A Sample of Interdialectal Conversation', in Charles A. Ferguson (ed.) Contributions to Arabic Linguistics (Cambridge, Mass., 1960), pp. 81-156.

15. Jean Cantineau, Le dialecte arabe de Palmyre (Beirut, 1934).

16. Yehoshua Blau, 'The Importance of Middle Arabic Dialects for the History of Arabic', Studies in Islamic History and Civilization, Scripta Hierosolymitana 9.206-28 (Jerusalem, 1961).

17. Charles F. Gallagher, 'The Language Problem in North Africa', North Africa: State and Society 1964 (18th Annual Conference of the Middle East Institute, unpublished papers).

BIBLIOGRAPHY

The following sources for the study of Arabic have been selected from the great mass of existing materials to provide readily available further reading, including beginning textbooks, on topics which are most likely to be of interest to American students of Arabic or to linguists. For convenience, very few periodical references are included and almost all works in foreign languages have been omitted.

A. CLASSICAL ARABIC

W. Wright, A Grammar of the Arabic Language, 3rd ed., 2 vols., Cambridge, Cambridge University Press, 1955. This is the basic reference grammar for Classical Arabic and has been a standard text for more than a century. It is rather cumbersome, leaning heavily on the Arab grammatical tradition.

Hans Wehr, A Dictionary of Modern Written Arabic, ed. J Milton Cowan, Ithaca, N.Y., Cornell University Press, 1961. A basic dictionary of the vocabulary in current use in the Arab world. Two other dictionaries are often recommended for beginning students:

Elias A. Elias, School Dictionary: Arabic-English, English-Arabic, Cairo, Elias Modern Press [no date]. Laconic and dated, but contains an English-Arabic section; and:

J.G. Hava, Arabic-English Dictionary, rev. ed., Beirut, Catholic Press, 1963. The best small dictionary for early Arabic and poetry.

There are a number of textbooks available, differing both in method and in the type of material they prepare the student to read, and more appear every year:

G.W. Thatcher, <u>Arabic Grammar of the Written Language</u>, New York, Frederick Ungar, [reprint ed., no date]. Several generations of Arabists started with this text and it remains the best text for a reading knowledge of pre-Modern Arabic. It has now been largely superseded by the following:

J.A. Haywood and H.M. Nahmad, <u>A New Arabic Grammar of the Written Language</u>, Cambridge, Mass., Harvard University Press, 1962. An inferior revised version of Thatcher which includes a great deal of contemporary vocabulary. Both Thatcher and Haywood and Nahmad are available with keys to the exercises.

More fashionable approaches emphasize the development of an active control of the language and usually presuppose the assistance of a native speaker and time spent listening to tapes. Texts of this genre include:

Farhat J. Ziadeh and R. Bayly Winder, <u>An Introduction to Modern Arabic</u>, Princeton, N.J., Princeton University Press, 1957 [records and tapes available].

Ernest N. McCarus and Adil I. Yacoub, <u>Elements of Contemporary Arabic: Part I</u>, Ann Arbor, Mich., Ann Arbor Publishers, 1962 [tapes available].

Daud Atiyeh Abdo, <u>A Course in Modern Standard Arabic</u>, 2 vols., Beirut, Khayats, 1962-64 [tapes available].

Charles A. Ferguson and Moukhtar Ani, <u>Lessons in Contemporary Arabic: Lessons 1-8</u>, rev. ed., Washington, D.C., Center for Applied Linguistics, 1964 [tapes available].

All of the texts include discussion of the Arabic script, but a more detailed treatment may be found in the following:

T.F. Mitchell, <u>Writing Arabic: A Practical Introduction to the Ruq'ah Script</u>, London, Oxford University Press, 1953.

Frank A. Rice, <u>The Classical Arabic Writing System</u>, Cambridge, Mass., Harvard University Press, 1959.

B. COLLOQUIAL ARABIC

Harvey Sobelman, ed., <u>Arabic Dialect Studies: A Selected Biblio-graphy</u>, Washington, D.C., Center for Applied Linguistics and the Middle East Institute, 1962. An evaluated list of sig-nificant scholarly work as well as textbooks published on the following dialects: Syrian, Egyptian, Arabian Peninsula, Iraqi, North African, and Maltese. Since publication of this bibliography a series of reference grammars and dictionaries have appeared in the Arabic Series of the School of Languages and Linguistics, Georgetown University, Washington, D.C.:

Richard S. Harrell, <u>A Short Reference Grammar of Moroccan Arabic</u>, 1962.

Wallace M. Erwin, <u>A Short Reference Grammar of Iraqi Arabic</u>, 1963.

Mark W. Cowell, <u>A Short Reference Grammar of Syrian Arabic</u>, 1964.

Harvey Sobelman and Richard S. Harrell, <u>A Dictionary of Moroccan Arabic: English-Moroccan</u>, 1963.

Beverly E. Clarity <u>et al.</u>, <u>A Dictionary of Iraqi Arabic: English-Iraqi</u>, 1964.

Karl Stowasser and Moukhtar Ani, <u>A Dictionary of Syrian Arabic: English-Syrian</u>, 1964.

The Moroccan-English, Iraqi-English, and Syrian-English volumes are forthcoming. The Series also includes introductory courses for two of these dialects (see below). Further sources for the dialects follow.

(1) <u>Syrian area</u>

Charles A. Ferguson with the assistance of Moukhtar Ani and others, <u>Damascus Arabic</u>, Washington, D.C., Center for Applied Linguistics, 1961 [reprint of materials developed in the fifties for the Foreign Service Institute].

Frank A. Rice and Majed F. Saʿid, <u>Eastern Arabic: An Introduction to the Spoken Arabic of Palestine, Syria and Lebanon</u>, Beirut, Khayats, 1960 [tapes available].

BIBLIOGRAPHY

(2) Egyptian area

T.F. Mitchell, An Introduction to Colloquial Egyptian Arabic,
    London, Oxford University Press, 1956.
Richard S. Harrell et al., Lessons in Colloquial Egyptian Arabic,
    rev. ed., 1963 (Georgetown Arabic Series [see above]) [tapes
    available].
Walter Lehn and Peter Abboud, Beginning Cairo Arabic, Austin,
    Texas, 1965 [order from Hemphill's Book Stores, Austin, Texas;
    tapes available].

Dictionaries present something of a problem for Egyptian Arabic.
The following are the most promising:
Socrates Spiro Bey, Arabic-English Dictionary of the Modern
    Arabic of Egypt, 2nd ed., Cairo, 1923.
-----, An English-Arabic Vocabulary of the Modern and Colloquial
    Arabic of Egypt, 3rd ed., Cairo, 1929.
Edward E. Elias, Practical Dictionary of the Colloquial Arabic
    of the Middle East: English-Arabic, 2nd ed., Cairo, 1949.

(3) Saudi Arabia

The Arabian American Oil Company has published in its Aramco
Arabic Language Series a number of texts and phrasebooks pri-
marily based on the dialect of al-Hasa on the east coast. The
vocabulary lists are the best available substitute for a dic-
tionary. The principal books in the Aramco series are:
Pocket Guide to Arabic, 1955.
Conversational Arabic [no date].
Basic Arabic, 1957.
Spoken Arabic, 1957 [accompanying records].
English-Arabic Work List, 1958.
Work Arabic, 1954- [a series of manuals dealing with technical
    vocabulary, e.g. medicine, transportation, etc.]

(4) <u>Iraq</u>

Merrill Y. Van Wagoner, <u>Spoken Iraqi Arabic</u>, 2 vols., New York, Holt, Rinehart & Winston, 1949 [records available].

Wallace M. Erwin, <u>A Basic Course in Iraqi Arabic</u>, forthcoming (Georgetown Arabic Series [see above]).

(5) <u>North Africa</u>

The great mass of publications on North African Arabic are in French and the few translations of text materials that have been made for particular programs are generally available, if at all, only in mimeographed form. For a survey of the literature see <u>Arabic Dialect Studies</u>, cited above. Only one modern text is widely available:

Richard S. Harrell <u>et al</u>., <u>A Basic Course in Moroccan Arabic</u>, 1965 (Georgetown Arabic Series [see above]) [tapes available].

(6) <u>Maltese</u>

There are two good introductory texts for Maltese: Aquilina is the more appropriate for the student with no knowledge of any form of Arabic, while Sutcliffe builds on a prior knowledge, drawing many comparisons:

E.F. Sutcliffe, <u>A Grammar of the Maltese Language with Chrestomathy and Vocabulary</u>, London, 1936.

Joseph Aquilina, <u>Teach Yourself Maltese</u>, London, English Universities Press, 1965.

V. Busuttil, <u>Dizzjunarju mill-Malti ghall-Inglis</u> [Maltese-English Dictionary], rev. ed., Malta, 1942.

<u>English-Maltese Dictionary</u>, Government of Malta, 1946.

C. ARABIC LITERATURE

There are a number of discursive histories of Arabic or other

BIBLIOGRAPHY

Islamic literatures which include extensive quotes from authors
discussed here, along with background material and bibliographies:

H.A.R. Gibb, Arabic Literature, 2nd ed., Oxford, The Clarendon
    Press, 1963.

R.A. Nicholson, A Literary History of the Arabs, Cambridge,
    Cambridge University Press, 1956.

Edward G. Browne, A Literary History of Persia, 4 vols.,
    Cambridge, Cambridge University Press, 1956. For Arabic,
    see especially vols. 1 and 2.

Arthur J. Arberry, Sufism: An Account of the Mystics of Islam,
    London, George Allen & Unwin, 1950.

Two sources of literary criticism and analysis should be mentioned
here as they go beyond the philological and historical study which
have been traditional:

H.A.R. Gibb, Studies on the Civilization of Islam, ed. S.J. Shaw
    and W.R. Polk, Boston, Beacon Press, 1962. See especially
    no. 7, 'Tarikh', an analysis of Islamic historiography; no. 12,
    'Reflections on Arabic Literature', a study of the development
    of Arabic prose style; and no. 13, 'Studies in Contemporary
    Arabic Literature'.

Gustav E. von Grunebaum, 'The Aesthetic Foundation of Arabic
    Literature', Comparative Literature 1952, pp. 323-40.

Lastly, there are many translations of whole works or of sections
of prose works brought together in anthologies. Only a very few
of these can be mentioned here.

Mohammed Marmaduke Pickthall, The Meaning of the Glorious Koran:
    An Explanatory Translation, Mentor Religious Classics, New
    York, 1958.

James Kritzeck, ed., Anthology of Islamic Literature, New York,
    Holt, Rinehart & Winston, 1964.

R.A. Nicholson, Translations of Eastern Poetry and Prose,
    Cambridge, Cambridge University Press, 1921.

A.J. Arberry, Modern Arabic Poetry, London, 1950.